Educating

By Vic Leigh

What happens in the office, doesn't always stay in the office.
A stand-alone book that will knock your socks off.

Educating Mr. B © 2024 Vic Leigh

All rights reserved. No portion of this book may be reproduced, stored in a retrieval system, or transmitted in any form or by any means—electronic, mechanical, photocopy, recording, scanning, or other—except for brief quotations in critical reviews or articles, without the prior written permission of the publisher.

Published in the United States of America

This book is a work of fiction. Names, characters, places, and incidents are the product of the author's imagination or are used fictitiously. Any resemblance to actual events, locations, or persons, living or dead, is coincidental. This book is intended for a mature audience of 18+. Adult content.

~ Dedication ~
To the man that I love:
Allen, you make my days so
Wonderful, I love you to the moon and back!
Thank you for all your support. You follow me to all my events, take me everywhere I need to go, make sure I have all the stuff I need, you are the very best!

Chapter 1

The Office of Emily VanZant, CFO, Nordic Software

"Get off my case, Chet. I don't care if you are the CEO of this fucking company. I make you money, and you don't want to let me go. Besides, I would file sexual harassment charges against you and fucking win." I'm fucking pissed at the moment. My boss and ex-boyfriend, Chet Griffin, is being somewhat of a persistent asshole.

Chet whines on the other end of the phone. "Come on, baby. You know..."

"Shut the fuck up, asshole. You don't have the right to call me anything but Ms. VanZant. I am strictly your employee now. Had I not caught you with your pants literally down around your ankles, with your new assistant sucking your dick, two weeks ago, it might be a different story. But here we are. Goodbye." I hang up the phone. Yeah, I caught him, in his office, with his new assistant, Ms. Treat. Appropriate name for the slut.

My assistant, Alexander Bennett, is sitting at his desk just outside my office. I'm sure he heard every word I said. He, of course, acts like he didn't hear anything.

My office is on the sixteenth floor of the Nordic Building in downtown Boise. I can look out my large picture window behind my desk and see Bogus Basin Ski Resort in the distance. In the wintertime, the resort is lit up at night. It's actually a beautiful sight. Boise is named for its many trees. However, the only trees you see are usually ones that were planted in the city. Boise is a desert and has dry winters with dry powder snow in the mountains.

I attended Boise State and received my Bachelor of Science degree in Business Administration. I then went on to acquire my Master of Business Administration. I didn't remember him being this much of an ass when we were in high school. Although, he was one of the snotty boys, and I was an average girl with no money. We did not hang out in the same social circles.

When he noticed me, I was walking through the Nordic reception area. Mr. Griffin made sure I learned all I needed to know to run the company. All Chet saw was a nice-looking blonde with big boobs and long legs. He didn't see that I had a mind. No, he wanted to fuck me on his desk after he hired me. I told him to go fuck himself.

About six months after I started working here, he promoted me to CFO. The man that had been here retired.

Chet asked me out, and we started dating. To my surprise, he was fucking every attractive girl in the company. When I confronted him about it, he said they were all jealous because we were dating, and nothing was going on with any of them. He still didn't remember me from high school, which I find quite funny. I don't dare tell him I was one of the poor girls who sat alone at lunch every day. He would never have talked to me about the job. What's even funnier, he has no idea what his dad and grandfather did to ensure the safety of the company once they were no longer here.

Last week, I went to his office to talk about a merger we have been working on with another smaller software company. His assistant, Ms. Treat, wasn't at her desk. She rarely was. I knocked on his door and walked in. I found out why she wasn't at her desk; she was on her knees and sucking my boyfriend's dick.

At first, I was shocked. Then, I started adding up all the times I saw him flirting with other women, and he would just blow it off. Now, I need to watch for those fucking red flags. I will not be used. I may use someone, but no one will use me like that ever again.

I watch my assistant, Alex. He reminds me of Superman—you know, Clark Kent—on that old TV show Lois and Clark: The New Adventures of Superman. What was that actor's name? Oh yeah, Dean Cain.

Alex has dark hair, wears wire-frame glasses, and has bulging muscles trying to escape his dress shirt. He always dresses professionally, wearing slacks and a dress shirt with a tie.

In this company, Chet requires that we all address each other using personal titles: Mr., Mrs., and Ms. His father started this company when the software was just becoming a huge thing, and Chet took over. Mr. Griffin required it, and so Chet has carried on that same tradition. To be honest, I think it's a power trip for him.

I clear my throat and say, "Mr. Bennett, could you come here, please?"

Alex walks into the room and carries a small notepad with him. He is very efficient and always carries something to write on. "Yes, Ms. VanZant."

"Have a seat." I have two large, comfortable leather chairs that sit in front of my desk.

He takes the one to the right.

I look at him for a moment. He's very nice to look at. I'm glad I hired him against Chet's wishes. "Mr. Bennett, you do understand that anything you hear or see in this office is confidential."

"Yes, ma'am." He looks at me, puzzled.

"Very well. I hope that you don't find the need to spread foolish gossip around the office to the other assistants," I continue.

He clears his throat. "Ms. VanZant, can I be frank with you?"

I smile, "Of course. I wouldn't expect anything else from my assistant."

He smiles back.

Fuck, I think my panties are wet.

"I really don't socialize with anyone from the office. Even if I did, I wouldn't tell them anything that is said in this office. First, it's none of their business. Second, I don't like gossips."

"Very well then. You've been here for about a year. How are you doing? Do you have any questions? Do I need to explain anything to you regarding..."

"No, I'm good. I have read all the financial statements for the company for the past five years. I am up to speed on what your job is. I think we are good."

I move a piece of paper on my desk as he talks. "Very impressive. I wanted to know if you could stay late tonight. I have some work that needs to get out by tomorrow morning and your help would be invaluable."

"Yes, ma'am. I'm always willing to help out where I'm needed." He stands. "Is that all you need?"

"That's it for now. Thank you." I watch as he turns and walks out the door and back to his desk. His ass must be made of steel. It's rock hard and so round. I want to bite it. But I can't, he's my assistant and fifteen years younger than me.

I can't be Chet and sexually harass my assistant. It's not right.

But I damn sure want to.

Chapter 2

Alex

I walk out of Ms. VanZant's office, wanting to go down the hall and beat the shit out of that scumbag ex of hers, *Mr. Griffin*. I feel like I'm back in school using Mr. and Ms. all the time. It's stupid. We are grown-ass adults, and we should be able to call each other by our first names.

Emily, Ms. VanZant, is a gorgeous woman. She didn't deserve to be treated like she was by that asshole. He needs to be knocked down a peg or two.

I look back at the beautiful blonde that is sitting at her desk, going through her computer. She wears reading glasses, which she has perched on her nose only when she's on the computer. Her light blonde hair falls below her shoulders in big curls. She wears one of those pencil skirts every day with a different color blouse. Her curves are enhanced, showing off her delectable ass.

I have got to get back to work. My dick is hard just fantasizing about my boss. How wrong is that? Very, very wrong. Okay, focus, get back to work.

Calming my dick down a bit, I adjust myself and return to my desk. I've got to get some work done.

Several hours later

Most of the office people had left for the day, and Ms. VanZant wanted me to stay late. I ran down to the office Café to get some snacks before they closed. When I got back to my desk, Emily was standing near it, waiting for me.

I look at her eyes because if I look anywhere else, my dick will certainly get stiff. "Can I help you, Ms. VanZant?"

"Oh good, I thought you had forgotten I needed you to stay over. Can you bring the Milton file, and let's go over a few things?" She smiles at me.

My brain says there is nothing to that smile but her being nice, but my twenty-five-year-old dick says there is way more to it than just a smile. Fuck!

I smile back, "Yes ma'am. I'll be right there. I was going to order pizza for dinner. What do you like?"

"Oh, I'm fine. I'll just grab something later." She walks back into her office.

I watch her as her ass sways back and forth, those heels of hers, fuck, I need a different boss. I shake the nonsense from my brain and grab the file she requested along with my notepad and pen.

She is bent over the front of her desk, and oh my God, I think I may have just come in my pants.

I look down to make sure there isn't a wet spot on the front of my grey slacks. Thank God there isn't.

Her ass has to be the best thing I've seen since Molly Porter let me touch her pussy in ninth grade. That's one I'll never forget. Molly Porter let everyone touch her pussy.

I clear my throat to let her know I've entered the office.

She straightens, "Oh, come on in. Don't be shy." She moves to the side of her desk, puts her hand on her desk, and lifts one foot, taking one of her heels off. Then, she does the same with the other. "I have no idea why women think we have to wear these God-awful things. They are the most uncomfortable pieces of shit made." Then she smiles at me and throws her shoes behind her desk.

I chuckle, "I guess that's why men wear sensible shoes."

"I think a man designed them because there is no way a woman would have. Okay, let's see that file. I think we have Mr. Milton by the balls on this one." She moves around her desk and takes a seat in her office chair. She moves her arm around, "Have a seat."

I sit in one of the leather chairs sitting in front of her desk. I try to get comfortable, but my dick doesn't seem to want to cooperate. As I watch Emily peruse through the file I handed her, my mind begins to wander.

I take my glasses off and set them on the desk. I move around to her side. I turn her chair so that I'm standing right in front of her, my dick right in front of her face. I slip her glasses from her nose and set them on top of the file.

Emily reaches up and unfastens my belt. Then she slides my pants down. She grabs the bottom of my shirt and rips it open, buttons flying all over the office. She looked at my crotch and licked her lips, never taking her eyes off mine. She smiles and then bites her bottom lip. She pushes my boxers down.

"I'm not sure this is appropriate Emily." However, I don't fight her on it.

Her eyes remain on mine as she starts to lower her mouth to my...

"Earth to Alex..." She snaps her fingers in my face. "Hello Alex! Are you with me?" Emily is sitting across the desk from me, and I am totally embarrassed about what I was just thinking.

I clear my throat, "Yes...yes, I'm here. I'm just...my thoughts were wandering. I apologize."

Emily takes her glasses off and sets them on the desk, and she clasps her hands together in front of her on top of the file. "Is there something you would like to talk to me about? You can ask me anything you know. We can talk about anything you need to talk about."

I'm pretty sure that my face is five shades of red. I shake my head, "Oh no, ma'am, I'm good. I just let my mind wander for a moment. What were you saying?"

Emily stands from behind her desk and walks around in front of me. She leans her ass on the desk and puts her hands on the desk on each side of her. "Alex, you seem a little uptight, are you worried about your job? Are you worried about anything here? Are you worried about me being your boss? I did ask you in the interview if you would have a problem working for a woman. And you said no. Is that still true?"

I stare at her for a moment. "Yes, ma'am, yes I...I'm good. I don't have a problem with working for a woman. I promise. I'm sorry; it won't happen again."

She bends at the waist and looks me in the eye. "If there is ever anything I can help you with, you let me know."

Well Fuck!

Chapter 3

Emily

I stand in front of Alex for several minutes. Watching his eyes try not to travel to my breasts is – in a word – captivating.

Standing straight, I run my hands down my skirt and smile my sweetest smile. "Alex, can I ask you a personal question?"

"Um, of course, anything," he stammers a bit.

I give him a brilliant smile, "You may regret saying that. But, I wonder what you like in women. I know this is very personal, and you don't have to answer. I find you very intriguing."

His eyes snap to mine, "I'm not sure that is something that we need to discuss at work. I mean it doesn't bother me, but should we be discussing things of that personal nature here?"

I walk back around to my chair. "No, probably not, but if you would like to discuss it, I'm open to that."

He clears his throat, seeming to think about what I said. Then he blurts out, "I like women who are straightforward, know what they want, and aren't afraid to ask for it." Then, he smiles at me—you know, that mesmerizing smile.

I stare at him and smile back. "That's interesting. I like a forceful man who goes after what he wants and is determined to get what he seeks. What do you seek, young Mr. B?"

He nods in agreement with me, rubs his hand across his stubbled jawline, and finally says, "I'm not sure."

The bulge in his pants tells me he likes our conversation. "Do you know what you want, Alex?"

His face turns a cute pink color. "I do."

"Make sure you always go after what you want," I say, licking my lips as I watch his eyes.

He gives me a smirk. "I plan on it."

This is the most inappropriate conversation in the workplace. I know this but shit, this man is hot, and I sure would like to...There is a knock at the door. *Shit!*

I just yell across the room, "Come in." I'm a little annoyed and frustrated, to say the least.

Chet walks in, "Hey, beaut..." he stops when he sees Alex sitting in the chair across from me. "What the fuck? Why is he in here with the door closed?"

I stand, cross my arms over my chest, and stare him down. "This is my office. You do not have anything to say when you are in my office. He's my assistant, he's going to be in my office, not that I have to explain myself. What do you want?"

"I was going to ask if you wanted to have dinner. Get rid of the kid and let's go have some fun." Chet starts toward my desk.

I stop him. "No, we are working on the Milton account. You can go now. I don't need anything from you."

He keeps walking toward me. "Come on, you can work on that in the morning. You'll be fine. You'll have Milton eating out of the palm of your hand." He reaches my desk.

I continue to stare him down and do not budge from my spot. "Chet, I will say this one more time. I do not have any interest in you anymore. We had our time and now it's over. You need to leave so we can get some work done."

"You do realize I own this company?" He puts his hands on his hips, pushing his suit jacket back.

"Oh, I remember. You do remember, I will file sexual harassment charges on you faster than you can turn around if you try to do anything to me or to Alex." I put my hands on my hips, and I'm furious.

10

"Who the fuck is Alex? This asshole? You call him by his first name? You know I have a strict policy on calling employees by their first names. Mr. Ben... Mr. B..., what the fuck is your name?" Chet turns his attention to Alex.

I stop Alex from speaking. "Alex, go get me some water please."

"Yes ma'am." Alex gets up from the sitting position that he's been in since he came into my office. Chet doesn't seem to faze him in the least.

I smile to myself as Alex makes his way out of the office. Then, I look at Chet. "Okay, asshole. Let's get this over with once and for all. I am not interested in you in the least. When I caught you getting sucked off by that last bimbo you hired, I was done. I will not, now nor ever, go out with you again. We are finished!" I yell. "We will not have anything but a professional relationship from here on out. You are not my boss, you are my equal. We were hired by the board as equals in this business. That was at your insistence. Now, get out of my office and don't bother me with this ever again." I move and sit down in my office chair, stare Chet in the eye, and don't back down.

Chet's face is red as a beet. "You will be sorry for this."

"I'm sorry I ever said yes to going out with you in the first place." I move the mouse on my desk and wake my computer. I ignore him as he leaves the office.

Alex is walking back in with a cup of water as Chet leaves.

Chet glares at him but doesn't say a word.

I look at Alex, "Thank you, I really didn't need..."

"I know. It's an empty cup." Then, he gives me that delicious smile. He walks in and shuts the door behind him. As he walks toward my desk, he doesn't stop at the chair where he was earlier. He walks around my desk to my side. He takes my hand, pulls me from my sitting position, and pulls me into him.

Fuck, his body is hard as a rock. "What?"

"Taking what I want." His lips are on mine fast and hard.

I can't help myself. I part my lips so he can plunge his tongue deep.

His kiss is slow, methodical, and amazing. It's like he is making slow, passionate love to my mouth. His hand goes into my hair and tilts my head slightly to the right, allowing him to delve deeper into my mouth.

Fuck! I feel my pussy throb. I don't stop him at first. Then, I finally come to my senses and pull away from him, a little breathless. "What was that for?"

He smiles, "You said to go after what I wanted. I think you want me as much as I want you."

"Alex, we have a working relationship." I stand straight, run my hands down the front of my skirt, and clear my throat. I look at him, a little confused because I so want to kiss him again.

"I'm sorry, maybe I misread the signals. I thought you wanted me as much as I wanted you." He starts to back up.

Shit! "Okay, maybe I did lead you to believe...you are like twenty-five. I'm way too old for a guy like you."

"You don't look or act older than me. You seem like a woman that sees what she wants and goes after it, regardless of a little age difference." He gives me that damn dimpled grin again.

Fuck!

He comes toward me again. "I locked the door as I came back in. No one can bother us."

I look at him with a surprised look. "Seriously, I'm forty. That's way to many years between us. You should be going out with a girl your own age."

He waves his hand, "Girls my age are worried about stupid shit. You are a woman with her shit together. I like that."

Am I really contemplating this? Fuck yeah, I am. He's hot. And from the bulge in his pants, he's very well endowed.

Fuck it! I walk toward him and pull him into me, "You ready for the ride of your life?"

"Bring it." His lips hit mine again, this time with a deep passion I didn't even know existed.

I wrap my arms around his waist, pulling at the hem of his shirt, as I press my breasts into his chest.

Alex is unzipping my skirt in the back.

I'm trying to get his shirt and tie off without strangling him.

Our mouth's part, we gasp for air, and each of us pulls at our clothes, trying to get them off faster.

My skirt falls to the floor, his shirt and tie are tossed to the side, his pants are undone, my shirt is undone, and my breasts are heaving.

We slam our mouths back together. I run my fingers through his thick, dark, wavy hair.

Alex grabs my ass with both hands and lifts me as our mouths devour each other.

I straddle him, wrapping my legs around his waist and my arms around his neck, and our worlds collide.

He pushes me against the wall behind my desk. His lips move from mine down my neck, nipping and sucking lightly on the tender spot as he makes his way to my earlobe. Alex sucks my earlobe into his mouth and bites it gently.

I moan. God, I need this. My back is against the wall, my legs wrapped around his waist. My hands are in his thick hair. And my head is thrown back against the wall.

He has one hand on my upper thigh, and the other moves to tenderly massage my breast. His hands are big, but not as big as my breasts. He massages and pinches my nipple hard, and his other hand squeezes my upper thigh. Alex removes his hand from my breast while he continues to kiss down my neck and across my shoulder.

I feel his dick at my entrance. I'm fucking dripping wet with excitement.

He stops everything, looks into my eyes, and says, "Are you sure this is what you want? I'll stop right..."

I put a finger over his lips, "I'm absolutely sure. Fuck me, Alex. Now!"

Alex's eyes turn dark, and he plunges his thick dick deep inside my pussy. His face buried deep between my shoulder and ear.

I gasp, then moan. "Fuck, this feels good. Right there, yeah, move just like that."

His hips are moving back and forth as his dick goes in and out of my wetness. He changes direction slightly, and his cock goes deeper with each plunge.

Young men are always eager to get finished.

This time, so am I.

I hold tight to his neck, my head back against the wall, and I'm panting as he continues to thrust in and out of my pussy.

"Fuck, your pussy feels so good. Emily, fucking come." He pushes harder and deeper.

My orgasm is inevitable. I squeeze my legs tighter around his waist as the warmth of satisfaction envelopes me, and I let go. "Fuck!"

He continues to push deeper as his release is ready to explode. "Fuck!" he lets go.

I feel his dick throb inside me. His warm cum slide down to my ass.

We hold each other for several minutes. Neither of us wanting to let go.

Alex finally pulls back, rakes a hand over my cheek, removing the hair stuck to it, leans in, and kisses me—a soft, gentle, lingering kiss.

I feel his dick slip from my wetness, and he pulls back from the kiss.

"That was amazing. Damn, you are perfect." He gently slides me down so that my feet carefully hit the floor. He's so gentle for such a big man.

I laugh, "I'm far from perfect." I start gathering my clothes that are thrown all over my office.

Alex does the same. "I certainly want to do that again."

I smile at him, "We'll see if we can't make that happen. Next time, maybe not in my office."

Things just might get complicated.

Chapter 4

Alex

The next day, I sit at my desk wondering why I fucked my boss. I'm an idiot. That's all there is to it. I'm stupid, and I'll have to find another job. You can't get mixed up with a woman at work. How many times do I have to repeat that in my head? A lot.

Don't get me wrong—Emily is amazing. But she's my boss—my older boss. She doesn't look older or act older, but it doesn't matter—she's older. I'm going to get fired. I just know it.

I stare at my computer screen and don't hear when Mr. Griffin comes through the office until he speaks.

"She in?" He glares at me.

"I'll let her know you're here." I pick up the phone and start pressing the intercom button.

Chet blusters, "No need." He proceeds to walk through Emily's office door.

Yep, I'm getting fired.

After a minute or so, I hear Emily yelling.

"Get out asshole, right now."

Then something crashes against the door.

"I said get out. You will never touch me again. I'll see to it that I am the last woman you touch."

The door to Emily's office swings open. Emily is standing there with her blouse half untucked.

I jump from my chair, "Are you okay? What happened?"

She's fuming, "Call security then the police. I want him arrested." She points behind her at Chet.

"What did he do?" I look between them.

"Just call security then the police, now." She's screaming and shaking.

Chet stands in the doorway of her office, a smirk on his face. "You'll get nowhere doing that. This is my company—mine, not yours. I do what I want here."

"Not any more asshole." Emily looks back at me.

I pick up the phone, dial the security line, and explain they need to get up there now. Then, I call the police.

Chet, still smirking, says, "You will bow to my wishes. I will see you on your knees before me. You will regret bringing in the police. I'll make your life hell." His voice is sinister and low, and he's almost glowing when he says those words to Emily.

I push Emily behind me, "Get out. Security is on their way up. The police are not far behind. You will not touch her again."

Chet laughs out loud, "You, pretty boy, are about to be looking for another job. Mark my words, I will have her, over and over again until she begs me not to stop."

I raise my fist back, and security rounds the corner to my office. I fail to punch the asshole but come close.

"Mr. Griffin, what seems to be the problem?" The head of security, Ned, asked.

Before Chet can answer, Emily says, "He attacked me in my office. I want him arrested. The police are on their way."

Ned's eyes grow three sizes. "Is this true?" He looked at Chet.

Chet blew it off and waved his hand around, "She'll say anything. I just fired her."

Emily starts after Chet, and I stop her. She screams at Chet, "That's a lie. You attacked me in my office. I have proof. You will not get away with this, you asshole."

"Mr. Griffin, I think you should go back to your office, and I'll take care of Ms. VanZant." Ned is nearly pushing Chet toward the elevator.

"I'm going." Then he looks at Emily and me, "You two, I want out of my building in less than an hour. You're both fired."

"You will not get away with this." Emily shouts as Chet steps onto the elevator.

Chet just smiles.

What the fuck just happened?

I watch as the elevator doors close, Chet smiling and looking back at us. I take Emily into her office with Ned right on our heels.

"Miss VanZant, I understand this is a difficult situation, but I do need to escort you and Mr. Bennett out of the building after you collect your personal things." Ned is standing by the door, watching both of us.

I look from Ned to Emily and say, "Gather everything you have that's personal. Whatever proof you have against Chet, get it."

Emily looks at me and scoffs, "I am not leaving this building. I'm waiting for the police to get here. Chet will be the one leaving the building."

Ned puts his hands on his hips. "Now Ms. VanZant, let's be rational about this. There's no need for the police to come. We can take care of this peacefully, just gather your things so you can leave the building."

Emily stares at him with her hands on her hips. "I will not leave this building, I have a right to be here. You have no idea who I actually am. I will have everything I need when the police arrive. I will not leave this building."

I watch her. There's something she has. I don't know what it is, but there is something she has that I feel will turn the tables on all of this.

Twenty minutes later, the police decide to show up. Ned lets them into the office and explains what happened.

There are three police officers. The one that looks like he's in charge speaks first. "Ms. VanZant, could you please explain to me why you won't leave the premises."

Emily reaches down and opens the bottom drawer of her desk, pulling out her purse. She reaches into the purse and retrieves an envelope. She hands the envelope to the police officer.

The policeman takes the envelope and opens it while looking at Emily. He looks over the papers that she's handed him. He looks back at Emily with a solemn face. "Could you explain to me why no one else knows about this? Including the man that called to have you removed from the premises."

Emily folds her arms over her ample chest. "It's simple. Chet's father, the real Mr. Griffin, knew that Chet would screw up this company and it would go under. He didn't want that to happen. I've known the family most of my life and I knew better than to get close to Chet, but I did. However, a year before Chet's dad passed away, he asked to meet with me. He had this document drawn up in case Chet did something stupid. This gives me legal authority to take over the company. He's sexually harassed at least four women. I have proof of that as well."

I'm standing there stunned. What the actual fuck?

The police officer asks Emily, "What do you want me to do?"

"Arrest Chet Griffin on four counts of sexual harassment. I would also charge him with misconduct in a work place. I will have the corporate stuff sent to the lawyers and they will file corporate misconduct. He's been embezzling money from the company for the past year. I can prove it, so don't ask." Emily has a very satisfied look on her face.

I'm about to burst out laughing. This can't actually be happening, can it? Damn.

Ned has been standing by me, and he looks at me, "I guess we have a new boss, son."

I smile, "Guess so."
Seriously, what the fuck just happened?

Chapter 5

Emily

I've been waiting for this day for over a year. Thank goodness I don't have to put up with that man any longer.

The officers leave, followed by Ned. I look at Mr. Bennett, "Do you think I'm nuts?"

He smiles that delectable smile, "Oh, no. I was so turned on during all that, I wanted to kiss you in front of everyone. So, what's your next step?"

"I have the lawyers forward everything to the District Attorney. There is more than enough to charge him with, and more. I've been collecting information, getting personal statements from the women he harassed, watched every penny he's been spending. He's going down and he needs to. His father was such a nice man. He wanted to help everyone." I look down at my desk and remember his father.

Charles W. Griffin was a real man. He was a devoted family man. He loved his wife more than life. It was fun watching them. I had a shitty family. Mr. Griffin was so nice to me and treated me like family.

I'm not sure when Chet became the true asshole that he is, but it was sometime while he was away at college. Chet went to Princeton. I went to the local state college in the next town over. I couldn't figure out why anyone would spend so much money on college, it's just a piece of paper showing you made it through four years of pure hell.

While Chet was off at college, I started working for Mr. Griffin. He brought me on as an intern financial assistant. My degree is in accounting with a minor in finance. Mr. Griffin didn't want Chet to know that he hired me. He said he had plans for me and not to let Chet know. So, I went through the entire interview with Chet knowing I was already hired. Mr. Griffin knew that Chet would screw up one day, and he wanted a backup plan.

My family life was less than perfect. My mom raised me, and I saw my dad when he had time for me. We lived paycheck to paycheck, and I vowed never to have to do that when I grew up.

When I met the Griffins, they were so nice and caring. I watched them closely because I'd never seen such a loving couple. Mr. G would help Mrs. G in the kitchen, he didn't have to, he said he wanted to. He hated being away from her because he loved her that much.

I watched the Griffins and realized I wanted that. I wanted a life where a real man wanted me and couldn't get enough of me—wanted to be with me twenty-four/seven—strived to get home just to see me. That's the kind of love I want, and that's what I've been holding out for.

I'm a forty-year-old woman, and I probably will never marry because I don't think those types of men exist anymore. Mr. G was a one-of-a-kind man.

"Emily...Emily...hey...you okay?" Alex's voice floats through the air.

I must have been spaced out in my thoughts and didn't realize it. "Yeah, I'm fine. I'm just thinking."

"What's your next move?"

Alex is leaning against the wall, watching me. His arms are folded over his very large muscular chest. His smile is infectious as he watches me.

I have to be very careful here. He does work for me. But I find him super attractive. Of course I do. He's a twenty-five-year-old man that just fucked me against my office wall. What the fuck was I thinking? I was thinking I hadn't had sex in a while; he was offering, and oh, did I want to. Seriously, nothing could come of it, though. He's way too young, and I'm sure he wouldn't want an older woman hanging around.

"We need to go to Chet's office. Let's see if they were able to get him out of the office without any issues." I walk toward Alex.

He pushes himself off the wall and stops me before I reach the door. He pulls me into him, runs his hand to the back of my neck, under my hair, puts the other on my hip, runs it around to my back, and pulls me in. He stares so intently into my eyes. "Emily VanZant, you are an incredible woman. I knew the moment we interviewed. I will do whatever you want me to do. You are something special." Then, his lips lightly land on mine.

I part my lips. My stomach does flip-flops, my brain shuts off, and my body reacts. I grab the front of his shirt and pull him to me.

His tongue slides into my mouth, roaming and exploring, soft and slow. Our tongues dance a beautiful dance, moving and swirling around. I feel as if he is making love to my mouth.

I moan softly. I can feel the effects of this kiss from the hardness pushing into my stomach. His dick is hard, and I know he wants me.

But at twenty-five, aren't most men's dicks hard like that? They stay hard until about thirty-five, and then it's gone. I've experienced that with an ex one time. It was so weird.

I dated a man, Bart Nickles, a few years ago. He was thirty-four, and I was thirty. He was great in bed, but that was the only thing he had going for him. I like sex, so I stuck around way longer than I should have. Anyway, we had sex every night for months and months. The night of his thirty-fifth birthday, we were messing around after dinner at my place.

Bart's dick would not get hard. He literally had limp dick. It didn't matter how hard I tried. It would not get hard. He was so embarrassed he got dressed and left the apartment.

I tried to call him several times over the next few days, and he never would answer.

He finally answered on the fourth day. "I just can't see you anymore. I have some things going on with work and I'm going to be super busy. I think it would be best if we part ways."

I am floored. I decide no more friends-with-benefits situations for me. I'm sure it was just a fluke, but men get so bent out of shape when their most prized possession doesn't work. I chalked it up to dating older men.

Alex pulls back from our kiss, puts his forehead on mine, and whispers, "I'll do anything to help you. Whatever you need, I'm there."

I smile, "Thank you." I pull back and look at him, "How long have you worked for me?"

He chuckles, "Almost a year. Why?"

"Have you always wanted to fuck me up against the wall in my office?" I have no expression on my face, and I look at his eyes.

He takes a step back, takes a deep breath, and starts speaking. "Emily, the day we met, my interview, I thought you were the most gorgeous woman I'd ever seen. I was trying to figure out how to not embarrass myself. I thought I was stumbling over my words during that interview. I wanted to, yes. My first thought was to bend you over the desk and take you right then and there. Then I got to know you. I got to know the real Emily. All sides, the good, bad, and ugly."

I look at him strangely, "Ugly?"

He laughs, "Yes. When you talk to your mom on the phone, you look like you are always in a fight within yourself. There's something she does to you that makes you feel bad. I don't put all the calls from her straight through. Because I know she upsets you. I don't like seeing you upset."

I stand back a little and look down at the floor. It is a coping mechanism growing up as a child. When mom would belittle me, that's what I would do. I learned that her words hurt more than any beating she could have given me. She was a cruel woman. She's a narcissist if I ever saw one. If it's not about her, it doesn't matter.

"I didn't realize that."

He put his hand on my cheek, "I watch you every chance I get. I will make sure no one hurts you. I promise."

"You're all of twenty-five, you don't need an older woman. You need someone your own age to have fun with. Go to parties. I'm over that scene." I back away, knowing I'm right.

He moves closer to me again. "Em, age is just a number. I don't care about age. I'm not a partier. I don't drink much. I did four years in the Marines, it taught me a lot. I'm a lot more grown up..."

"Wait, how did I not know you were in the Marines? It wasn't on your resume." I'm shocked.

He smiles, "I don't put it on there because people look at me differently. I'm just me; there is nothing wrong with me. I just didn't re-up when it was time. I was done "seeing the world." I had to go overseas, but I didn't see anything bad. It wasn't at all what I thought it was going to be. I got my degree while I was still in the Corps."

I'm stunned. I stare at him until my phone rings. I retrieve the phone, "Ms. VanZant."

While I listen to Ned on the other end of the line tell me all that went down with Chet, I haven't taken my eyes off Alex.

What the hell is he up to, and why am I so attracted to him?

Then Ned says something that blows my mind.

"What did you just say?"

Chapter 6

Alex

The look on Emily's face goes blank, and she turns white as a ghost. I walk closer to her desk, not taking my eyes off hers.

All she says is, "Did anyone get hurt?" and "Keep me posted." She hangs up her phone.

I look at her, "What? What happened?"

"Chet, he went crazy as soon as they said he was being arrested. He pulled a gun on the police. Ned backed out of the office and called me. Is he that unstable that he pulls a gun on the cops?" She looks perplexed. Then, she picks up the phone, "Clear the building. Start with Chet's immediate area. Make sure no employees get hurt."

I walk around the desk, pull her up from her chair, and into my arms. "What do we need to do?"

She shakes her head, "I guess I should leave the building. But I need something from my safe first. Hang on." She walks to the bathroom just off her office. She's gone for a few minutes and then returns. "Okay, let's go."

After we gather whatever we can, laptops, phones, her purse, and the files she has, we leave her office. We head down the back stairway and hit the ground floor in just a few minutes. We walk to the parking garage.

She looks at me, "I'll text you my address. We'll go there for now."

"What if he gets loose? He'll know to go there. Let's go to mine. I'll text you my address and we'll meet there." I pull my phone from my pocket, text my address, and nod at her.

"Wait, I need to make sure all the employees get out and are safe." She starts for the street in front of our building.

I stop her, "No, Ned can make sure they all get out, and he will tell them to go home."

Her eyes are big and beautiful, "Okay, I'll call Ned from the car. I'll meet you at your place."

I nod and head for my car after I make sure she gets in hers.

What the fuck was he thinking? Chet has never been a violent person. Why on earth would he pull a gun on anyone? Especially the police. Several scenarios run through my head as I make my way across town.

My apartment is in a high-rise on the upper east side of the city. It's a nice place; I like my comfort. What got my attention was the full workout room in the basement. It's a perk of living in the building. I don't have to go out to the gym anymore.

I park in the garage to the east of the building. As I park in my usual spot, I spot Emily's car pulling in. She pulls in a few spaces down from mine. Getting out of my car, I wave at her, and she comes right over.

"You know, I can help with some of that stuff." I try to pull some of the things from her arms.

"I've got it. If you try to get anything, I'll probably lose everything." She is one headstrong woman.

I motion to the elevator, "This way then. What did Ned say when you called back?"

"They finally got all the employees out. They were told to go home, and we'll contact them as soon as we can. They finally got Chet down and cuffed and are currently on their way to the police department to book him." She follows me into the building.

I push the button for the twenty-sixth floor.

She smirks, "Twenty-six, is that the top floor?"

I nod, "Yes it is. It's got the best views of the city."

When the elevator doors open, I help her out with all of her stuff, and she follows me to my apartment at the end of the hall. I open the door and allow her to go in first.

She stops dead in her tracks at the entrance.

I look at her, "What's wrong?"

Emily looks over at me, "How much do I pay you? This is nice."

I laugh, "I have money. You don't pay me that much."

The space is open and inviting. When you walk in the door, the living area is to the left, and the dining/kitchen area is to the right. The living room has large leather furniture, with a sofa, a loveseat, and two recliners adorn the space. The dining room has a large wooden pedestal table that seats six with the option to seat ten and a beautiful China cabinet that matches. It's very comfortable, and the open concept is fantastic. It's bright and airy. A huge window in the living room overlooks the city of Boise, so beautiful. There's a hallway beyond the living room that leads to two bedrooms and two bathrooms. The rooms are super huge, and the bathrooms are a good size as well.

"Make yourself at home. Would you like a drink?"

She looks at me as she sets her things down on the dining room table. "What do you have?"

"Beer, wine, soda, your pick," I open the fridge.

"A nice glass of wine would be great right now." She pulls her shoes off and lays them on the floor near a chair at the dining table. "Oh man, that feels good."

I laugh, "Why do women insist on buying stupid shoes if they hurt their feet?"

She looks at the discarded shoes, "Because they are pretty and go with my outfit."

I scoff, "so you give up comfort to look good. I can look good and be comfortable in a pair of fifty-dollar sneakers."

She rolls her eyes.

I walk over to her after pouring her wine and hand her the glass of a nice burgundy.

"Thank you, I hope this calms my nerves. Chet is an asshole. Which I knew when I agreed to date him. But his grandfather loved me. So much so, he gave me the company when Chet proved to be the stupid ass that he is. His grandfather didn't like Chet much. He thought him to be an entitled asshole." She smirks, "He is and I hate him for it."

Chapter 7

Emily

My phone rings as I take a sip of my delicious wine. "Hello."

A female voice is on the other end. "Ms. VanZant, this is Detective Joy Penrod. I'm leading the investigation into Mr. Chet Griffin's criminal actions regarding the embezzlement charges and firearms charges. Can I come by and visit with you? Get some more information?"

I shake my head like she could see me. "Yes, I'm at my assistant's place." I rattle off the address and hang my phone up. I look at Alex, "Detective Penrod is coming by to ask me some questions. I hope you don't mind."

He shakes his head, "absolutely not. You can do whatever you need to do."

I move toward Alex, "Thank you." I put my hand on his hard, massive chest. "You are a lifesaver. Thank you for everything." Then, I tip-toed up and kiss his lips gently. It's a thank-you kiss, not a passionate one.

Alex is such a gentleman. He puts his hands on my shoulders, smiles, and whispers, "I'd do anything for you—anything at all, minus killing someone."

Laughing, I add, "But you'd help me bury the body, right?"

"Absolutely," he pulls me into him and just holds me.

This is what I needed. I just needed to be held comforted.

Finally pulling away, I look at him. "I need to use the restroom before the police arrive."

"Sure, this way."

I follow him down the hallway to a beautifully decorated bathroom.

"Here you go. If you can't find something, just let me know, I've got everything a woman might need." He smiles and walks back down the hall.

I move into the bathroom, close the door, and look at myself in the massive black framed mirror hanging on the wall above one of the double sinks. My face is red and blotchy. I have little to no makeup left on, and my hair is a mess.

Moving my hand down my hair, trying to straighten it out, I decide it's no use. I open a drawer on the large vanity, in it, there are combs, brushes, and a hairdryer. "Bingo."

Why on earth would he have so many things for a woman? I let that thought slide by. I grab the comb and manage to make my hair look a little more presentable. After replacing the comb, I shut the drawer and open the next one. There are several liquid makeup containers of various shades. Why? I have no idea, and I'm tired and don't care at the moment. I retrieve some of the makeup that looks to be close to my shade and apply a small amount on my face.

Once I've finished, I look again in the mirror. "Much better." I use the toilet, wash my hands, and leave the bathroom.

When I get close to the living room, I hear voices. The detective must be here. When I round the corner to the living room, a nice, attractive young woman is standing in a pair of dark blue slacks, a white button-down shirt, and a dark blue blazer over it. Her shoes are black and look very comfortable.

Alex is smiling and laughing with the woman, which makes my stomach do flip-flops. What could they possibly be talking about? It's as if he knows the woman, or is he flirting with her?

I shake my head again and walk into the room. "Good afternoon."

The two turn and smile at me.

Alex came over to me, "This is Joy. I mean Detective Penrod." He laughs and takes my hand, pulling me toward the woman.

Joy Penrod has a beautiful head of deep dark brown hair, her eyes are a caramel color, and her figure is that of a model. When did the police department get such beautiful women to work for them? She should be on the runway.

I stick out my hand, "It's nice to meet you Ms. Penrod."

She corrects me, "Mrs. I was just telling Alex that I got married last month."

"Really, that's wonderful. Congratulations. Um, do you two know each other." I'm a bit confused because Alex is somewhat familiar with this woman.

Alex laughs, "Yes, we went to high school together. She married one of the guys I hung out with. I've known Joy since we were in middle school."

I smile at them both and turn my attention to Joy, "That's wonderful. You are really young to be a detective."

She laughs, "After high school, I went to West Point for two years. When I graduated early, I wanted to come home and be a cop. So, I did. I made detective in record time. I assure you, I do know what I'm doing, and I will handle this case with the utmost professionalism. You don't need to worry about that."

I give her a strange look, "You went from West Point Academy to being a detective for the local police department? That is not a normal career move, is it?"

"No ma'am. I wanted to come home and be with Jerry. The logical choice was to be on the police force. With my training at West Point, I became a detective in a year. I'm the youngest ever detective with the Boise Police Department." She looks at me with a stern face, "I will do my job, Ms. VanZant. I will make sure that Mr. Griffin pays for his crimes. Do you mind answering a few questions for me?"

"Thank you for making me feel a little better and yes, you may ask me anything you need to ask. I need to make sure Chet pays for everything he's done."

Alex put his hand on the small of my back. "Shall we sit?" He motions to the tan leather sofa on the opposite side of the living area.

His living room was massive, and the furniture matched.

We move to the sofa, and the detective moves to one of the two chairs that match the sofa across from us. A table is sitting between us.

Alex asks, "Can I get anyone anything to drink?"

Joy looks at him. "Water if you have it. I can drink tap water. I'm not a prima donna who needs bottled water."

They both laugh.

Alex looks at me, "Do you want your wine?"

"Yes please, that would be great."

Then he leaves the room.

I glance back at the detective, "So, Detective Penrod, what do you need to know?"

She smiles, "Call me Joy. Let's start at the beginning."

Two hours later, Joy finishes asking questions. She stands from the chair, stretches a bit, and sticks her hand out to shake mine. "If you need anything, remember anything, let me know." She pulls out a card from her jacket pocket and hands it to me. "Call me at this number if you need me. I'll be in touch."

We follow Joy to the door, and she leaves.

I look at Alex, "So, that was interesting. I had no idea it was going to take so long to explain what a piece of shit Chet is."

Alex rubs my shoulders slightly, "Yeah, come on. Are you hungry? I'll fix you something to eat."

I start to walk toward the kitchen. "I am a little."

Moving into the kitchen, Alex pulls some things from the fridge. His tight ass is on full display. Maybe we can do something else before we eat.

"Hey, you know I might be hungry for something else right now," I smile as he lifts the food from the fridge.

He gives me a 'like what' look.

I move to where he is standing, smile, and lick my lips. I move my hand to the waistband of his dress pants, undo his belt, and slide them down his legs.

"Oh, you're that kind of hungry." He laughs and moves to take his shoes off so that his pants can be kicked off and pushed out of the way.

The bulge in his boxer briefs is mighty impressive. He pulls his shirt up over his head and tosses it to the side.

I lick my lips again, slide down to my knees, and pull his boxers down, freeing his massive cock. I move my tongue around the head of his dick, licking the pre-cum, while I massage his balls.

He moans in delight, and his hands make their way to my hair, gripping it from both sides.

I begin to move my mouth up and down his shaft, swallowing as the head hits the back of my throat, giving him a tickling sensation. The faster I move, the tighter the grip he has on my hair. He begins to pull at it. I feel his balls tighten some, and I pop off the head of his dick, making a popping noise with my mouth.

"Oh my God! What was that?" He let out a moan.

"I wasn't ready for you to come yet." I stand and begin taking off my clothes slowly. Enticing him, "See anything you like?" I toss my bra to the side and remove my skirt.

"Oh yeah." He begins to move toward me, and I back up.

"Not yet," I wiggle my finger back and forth in the no-no wave. "You must be patient."

He let out a sigh, "You nearly make me shoot my load down your throat and stop. Now you are torturing me by not letting me fuck you. Come on."

I smile, slowly remove my panties, and back up a bit more. "You want me, come get me." I turn and take off out of the kitchen, running. I should have thought this through. This is not my house, and I have no idea where I'm going. I head down the hallway. There has to be a room I can duck into.

I hear him hot on my heels, chasing me down the hallway.

Just as I'm about to escape into a dark room, an arm wraps around my middle, pulling me into the hard wall of a man.

I giggle, "How did you catch me so fast?"

His hot breath is at my ear, "I'm just faster than you." Then, he bit at my earlobe, sucking it into his mouth. "You wanna play? Let's play."

With his free hand, he snakes it around to my stomach and moves his fingers down, finding my clit. He pushes, then manipulates the little nub.

My legs become weak, my head goes back against his chest, and I moan. My hands reach around behind him, planting both palms on each of his solid ass cheeks, and I squeeze.

Alex holds me tight to his body as he continues to play with my engorged clit. His hot breath near my ear, "You like that, don't you. Wanna come?"

"Yes," I breathe out softly, desperately needing him to make me feel better.

I feel his lips curve up near my ear, then his hand moves from my clit, and his wonderful fingers are gone. "Wait, what are you doing? I need to come."

He spins me around, smiling down at me and pulling me close. " I'm just following the leader. You didn't let me come, so I didn't let you come."

I bite my bottom lip, "So now what? I really need to come, my insides are shaking."

Alex laughs, lets me go, grabs my hand, and pulls me into the room I was just about to enter. He hits a button, and a few lamps come on, illuminating the room slightly but not too much.

Inside his room is a massive four-poster bed, big enough for four people to fit on. A dresser is on the wall to the right. Giant floor-to-ceiling windows across from the bed, taking up most of the wall and overlooking god knows what, two end tables on each side of the bed, and a nice fluffy dark tan rug under the bed that spans out at least four feet from the edge.

"Nice room."

He points to a closed door on the left, "That's the bathroom, the closet is in the back of the bathroom." Alex pulls me back into his gorgeous chest and slams his mouth over mine. His tongue plunges into mine, taking me by surprise.

I'm not much on being dominated. I'm usually the dominating one, but what he just did turned me the fuck on and fast.

One of his hands moves down my side and around to my ass, cupping one cheek, his tongue is moving like he's searching for something, and then I find myself pushed away and thrown onto the bed.

Gasping, I mutter, "What the hell?"

"You like it rough don't you? I'm not sure I know how to be rough, but I'll give it a try." His eyes grow darker as he hovers over me.

"Who said I like it rough?" I exclaim.

Alex tilts his head to one side, looks me in the eye, and says, "You do. I know you do. I think you are used to being in charge in the bedroom as much as in the board room. Maybe you can teach me a thing or two. I've only been with two other women in my life."

"You're only twenty-five, you've got time. You seem to be a quick learner." I run my hand down his chest, "I might have a few things I can teach you. We'll have to be at my place though."

"But for now, I'll do my best to satisfy you."

Alex moves over me, spreads my legs with his knees, and plunges his dick deep inside my pussy.

"Fuck!" I fist the blankets with both hands and bow my back as he thrusts over and over into my wet center. "Fuck...fuck...fuck!" My legs wrap around his back, locking my ankles to pull him in deeper.

Alex looks down as he pounds his cock inside me over and over. "You like that, don't you. You like my big cock inside you."

All I can manage to get out is, "Yes." My hips are meeting each of his thrusts, making his dick go deeper. "Fuck, yes!"

"I'm coming, come with me Em, fucking come!" Alex yells out as we both hit our climax at the same time.

I squeeze my eyes shut and see stars as my release meets his.

Two people enjoying each other's bodies is an amazing, euphoric feeling. My brain shut off for a minute before regaining my equilibrium. When I open my eyes, Alex is still above me, brushing my hair off my face and watching me.

He gently runs his hand up and down my side.

I release my legs from his waist, but he doesn't move.

He just stares into my eyes and continues running his hand up and down my body. His breathing has returned to somewhat normal.

On the other hand, I'm still breathing hard and trying to catch my breath. How is he not breathing hard? He just did enough work to run a marathon. I watch his eyes; they turn softer and stay focused on me.

I finally get my breathing calmed down enough. "That was amazing."

He smiles, "Yes it was. I've got a lot to learn, but I'm up for the challenge if you are."

I laugh, "Oh really."

Still smiling, he says, "Oh yeah." He kisses my nose, slides his dick from my pussy, and moves to my side, lying on his back.

I clear my throat. It's getting a bit real here. "I need to use the restroom." I say, starting to move from the bed.

He stops me, "I don't know how all this will work, I'm not even sure I want this to go anywhere, but you are fucking amazing. I had no idea a woman could be so...sexual."

I smile, "I'll be right back." I can't say anything else. *He's not sure he wants it to go anywhere? I'm sexual?* As I walk to the bathroom, I think to myself, I always get what I want, and I want him.

Finishing up in the bathroom, I look in the mirror. Now what? Do I leave? Does he want me to stay? I shrugged. I guess I'll see what happens.

Walking back into the bedroom, Alex is lying on the bed under the covers. He pulls back one side of the blankets, offering me a chance to slide in next to him.

When I lie down, he covers me up, pulls me in to his side, and we cuddle.

I don't usually cuddle, but his arms around me feel so nice.

He leans into my ear and whispers, "After the day we've had, let's get some rest. I know I'm tired, you must be exhausted."

When I look into his eyes, I see an innocent boy. He's so much younger than me. Why would I be so attracted to a guy who is so young? All I could say was, "Yeah, I'm exhausted."

He kisses me gently on the lips, "Rest. We'll face whatever we need to, tomorrow."

The next thing I know, my eyes close, and I feel...comfortable. I am being taken care of for a change. I'll let it happen just this once. I'll sleep and then go home in the morning. Tomorrow is another day. I'll worry about everything tomorrow.

The next thing I know, I'm drifting off to sleep.

Chapter 8

Alex

Waking up, I reach for Emily, but she isn't there. I get out of bed and head for the dresser, pulling out a pair of my grey sweatpants and putting them on. I walk down the hall and smell the distinct aroma of coffee. "Em, where are you?"

Emily is standing in my kitchen, stark naked, holding a coffee cup. "Good morning." She gives me her million-dollar smile.

"Well, good morning to you, too. How long have you been awake? You should have woken me." I move toward her with a smile on my face. You look really good." I pull her toward me, and she sits her cup down on the counter.

"I thought you might want to sleep in a bit." She moves into my arms, kisses me, and then pushes me away. "Do you want some coffee?"

I chuckle, "You and your coffee. Yeah, I'll have a cup." I take a seat at the island across from where she is pouring the coffee.

She glances over her shoulder before finishing the coffee, "How'd you sleep last night?"

I give her my best smile, "Better than I have in years. How about you?" I'm watching her ass, such a beautiful ass.

"Great! I usually don't sleep well in strange places, but I felt right at home. Thank you for that." She turns her glorious nakedness toward me and hands me a cup of coffee. "Here you go."

I watch her as she floats across my kitchen in all her nakedness. She really is one fine woman. I don't care how old she is. I take a sip of my coffee. "You look really good this morning."

Emily smiles from behind her coffee cup, her eyes dancing in the glow of the kitchen light. "Thank you. I'm hoping I can go back home tonight. I'd like you to see where I live. I actually would like to show you something."

Now my curiosity is piqued, "Oh, what might that be?"

"You'll see. I do, however, have a serious question for you."

I sit my cup down on the counter, "Okay. Shoot."

She sets hers down as well, puts her hands on the bar, and stares at me briefly before she speaks. "I know that the age difference bothers you. I can see it in your eyes. I'm quite a bit older than you. Where do you see this going? Or do you see it going anywhere? Maybe I'm jumping the gun here, sorry. Disregard what I just said. I'm going to go get my clothes on..."

"Emily, wait." I jump up to catch her before she leaves the room. I grab her by her wrist. "Hold on a minute." Her naked body is really starting to get to me, and my dick stands at attention. Damn, asshole. "I wanted to talk to you about all that as well. I was going to wait until the Chet issues were finished. Let's get a shower and clothed, then we can talk. How does that sound?"

She nods, "Sure. But do you want to do something about that," she points to my ever-growing dick and smirks.

I shake my head, "Later. As much as I would love to stay tangled in the sheets all day with you, I think we need to get these other matters resolved first."

"I agree," she goes before me down the hallway.

I follow her to my room and pull her into my bathroom ensuite. I start the shower and grab some towels. Hanging them on the hooks near the shower doors I begin to get rid of my sweats. I pull her into the shower with me.

We just let the water flow over us and explore each other's bodies. I am trying to memorize every part of her in case one day she decides she doesn't want a young ass guy anymore. I want to savor every minute I can with this woman.

We apparently can't keep our hands off each other. After showering and screwing our brains out during said shower, we get ready and head into the office.

We decide to take Emily's car and ride in together. As we are heading down the road, her phone rings.

"Emily VanZant."

Ned's voice comes over the car radio system, "Ms. VanZant, I'm sorry to bother you so early, but we've had a development in Mr. Griffin's issue."

"What's the issue, Ned?" Emily is as cool as a cucumber.

He clears his throat, "He's here. He said he was out on bond and wants in his office. I've explained to him that he is not allowed in at this time. What do I do?"

"I had his key card disabled last night, so how did he get into the building?" Emily looks confused.

"I'm not sure. But I think the receptionist is a *fan* of his." Ned says the word fan like it is a dirty word.

"I'll take care of her when I get there. I'm on my way." She accelerates faster.

"See you soon, then." Ned disconnects the phone.

Emily speaks to her car, "Google, call Butler, Stone, and Reeves."

"Calling Butler, Stone, and Reeves, Attorney at Law." Her Google app repeated it.

She looks over at me, "Sorry, this may get a bit hairy."

I shrug, "No problem."

"Butler, Stone, and Reeves, how may I help you?" a voice says over the line.

"This is Emily VanZant with Nordic Software. I need to talk to Joe Stone, please." She's so calm.

"One moment please." There are a few clicks.

Several seconds later, a male voice comes over the line. "Emily, what can I do for you?"

"Joe, Chet is at the office causing issues. He apparently got out on bond. Can we get something to keep him away from the building?"

Joe is silent for a second. "I can request an injunction. Due to ongoing criminal charges regarding the company, the judge should grant it. I'll get this done right now. You'll hear back from me by noon. In the meantime, call the police and have him escorted from the building."

"Thanks, Joe. I'll do that."

Joe continues, "I did receive all of the documents you sent over yesterday. I've sifted through most of it. It's quite clear cut. The company now belongs to you. I'll get that paperwork started as well. It should be a simple transfer of titles."

Emily takes a deep breath, "That would be awesome. Thanks so much."

"You're welcome. I'll be in touch." Joe hangs up the phone.

I finally say, "How can you be so calm?"

"Why blow up? That would be no good for anyone. I have to stay calm. Chet will be escorted off the premises, again. I'm sure he'll try to retaliate in some way, but I have the law on my side." She pulls into her parking spot in the underground garage to the building, turns to me, and says, "I don't have the luxury of blowing up. I must stay calm in all matters regarding the company. I'm now in charge and I need to keep my head about me. Can you?"

I look at her for a minute, perplexed. I clear my throat before answering. "Yes, I think I can. I'll just follow your lead."

"Good." She nods her head up and down. "Now, let's go to work."

We both get out of the car and head for the elevator to the top floor.

Chapter 9

Emily

The elevator doors open, and a small army stands around a man, Chet. I make my way through the crowds, look back at Alex, and say, "Get everyone out except the police."

He nods to me and does as I ask.

There are six officers: Ned, our head of security, and Chet.

I step close to the officers but don't go beyond. I look at Chet, "What do you want, Chet? Why are you here?"

Chet laughs loudly, then screams at me, "This is MY company. How the hell did you get MY company?"

I try to speak softly. "Chet, your dad and grandad decided that the direction you were heading early on, was not what they thought they wanted for this company. They met with me, secretly and wanted me to head the company if and when you derailed."

"Wow! My family really had high hopes for me. What the fuck? This is so messed up. They give MY company to a perfect stranger." He's yelling and pointing, spit flying from his mouth.

"Chet, let the police officers take you. Go with them. Your attorney can give you all the details. It's perfectly legal." I move back and look at the officer closest to me. "Take him."

All six police officers literally tackle Chet to the floor.

Chet is not going quietly. He is yelling and screaming that he'll get me back for stealing his company.

After putting the cuffs on Chet's wrists, they pull him to his feet. Chet looks at me as they remove him from the office. He glares at me and fucking spits at me.

Thank goodness I am far enough away that he missed me.

Once the officers had Chet on the elevator, I texted Alex to let him know that the employees should come back to their offices in ten minutes, not a moment sooner.

Alex: Yes ma'am
Me: Come to the CEO's office when you are finished.
Alex: Will do, see you soon.

A smile spreads across my face as I put my phone back into my purse and head to the office that is now mine. Before we can move forward, I'll have to find where Chet is in some business dealings. That shouldn't be too hard since he hasn't been working on much lately. He'd been playing more than working over the past six months. I'll get things back on track.

This is not what I want to work on today, but here goes.

I move to the massive mahogany desk that Chet insisted on having after his dad passed. I walk slowly around it, running my finger across the smooth, dark wood as I walk around the perimeter.

Why did Chet lose it? Why is he acting like a spoiled brat?

I hear people moving outside the office and heading back to the outer space. Once everyone is back upstairs, I motion to Alex to help me.

Alex steps up to my side. "What do you need?"

"A place to elevate me so that everyone can see me and hear me. I need to address this group of people now. We'll need to set up a formal meeting for everyone later today."

Alex nods and pulls a table about knee-high over to where I am standing. Then, he takes my hand and helps me get on top of the table. Alex raises his voice slightly, "Could I have everyone's attention, please?"

All the employees' eyes find Alex's voice and then see me standing on the table.

I smile. "Could everyone come a little closer? I would like to talk with you briefly."

The twenty or so employees move so that they can hear me.

"Thank you all for your patience. I know you want to know what is going on. I will tell you. Chet Griffin is no longer a part of Nordic. I will be replacing him as the CEO. Chet has done some questionable things over the past several months. If you have helped or contributed to what he was up to, I'll be getting with you soon. You should not worry about your job at this point. If you are loyal to Nordic, then you will be loyal to me. If you were loyal to Chet, that is another issue. I want the best for Nordic and its employees. If you would like to speak with me, please get with Mr. Bennett to set up a time. I want to speak to you all as soon as possible. We will be meeting with the entire staff later this afternoon. Please return to work. Again, if you want to speak to me first, see Alex immediately. Thank you all so much for your loyalty and time."

The employees who had gathered around went back to their desks and began to work on whatever they were working on before I interrupted them. Of course, the whispers and rumors had already started.

Alex raises his hand to help me down from the table. We go to my office, and he shuts the door. "You okay?"

"As okay as I can be. Chet is an asshole, and he's lost all sense of reality." I lean my ass against the desk.

Alex comes up close to me, but not too close. "Now what?"

I shrug, "No idea. I guess see where we are here. Move all my things to this office and see what needs to be done on the corporate stuff. The board wants to meet with me this afternoon. Could you schedule that for me? Two PM."

"Absolutely. I'll get the things that we need to move from office and get those over to his. What about his secretary?"

I sigh, "she is another casualty of Chet's fuck ups. Let's see if she has any skills other than sucking dick. She may be moved to another area."

Laughing, I reply, "You have a way with words Ms. VanZant."

"Thank you, Mr. Bennett. Now, let's get moving." I stand and go to my office to begin packing my things.

Alex leaves the office to do his part of the moving.

What a fucking way to start my day...DAMN!

Well, today has been a hell of a day. Alex and I moved everything from my office to Chet's office. We have fielded phone calls from everybody, from the press to my mother, whom I did not speak to.

The board meeting was as expected. They named me CEO of Nordic. Now, I have to find a new CFO.

I heard from the attorney, and Chet's bail has been denied.

I finally get to sit at my new desk and breathe.

My ass barely hit the seat, and somebody knocks on my door. Who the fuck could that be? "Come in."

Alex's head pops around the door as he opens it. "I know you've got to be hungry because you haven't eaten all day. What do you say, you take the rest of the afternoon off, and let's go get some food."

I look at my watch, and it is 4:00. I look back at Alex, "That sounds like a great idea to me. What do you want to eat?"

"Oh no, ladies' choice. You can have anything you want, name it, and we'll go get it. If you want to order something and pick it up and go to your place or my place we can do that if you want to go to a restaurant, sit down we can do that..."

I raise my hand and stop him in his mid-word vomit. "I would rather not have to go into a restaurant. Let's figure out something to eat that we can take home, and we'll go back to my place."

Alex smiles, walks into the office, and says, "Perfect I'll call it in what do you want."

I put my hands under my chin and reply, "Pasta sounds good. From Luigi's. We can stop on the way to my house."

"Perfect. Caesar salad, right?"

I nod my head in agreement.

Alex gives me his brilliant smile and takes off out of the office.

I think of all the different kinds of things I can do to that boy. Just wait until I get him home.

Chapter 10

Alex

After we stop to pick up the food, we head to Emily's house. She lives in a gated community on the north side of Boise. We pull up to the gate, and she gives me her code, which I punch into the keypad. Then, the gate opens. We drive down a nice street filled with beautiful homes.

Emily gives directions, and we wind around the subdivision until we reach the backside, where her house sits on top of a hill. As I pull into the driveway, I look at the enormous stucco home. It can't be more than two or three years old.

I look over at Emily and ask, "this is where you live?"

She shrugs, "I like nice things. Come on." She opens her door and gets out.

I open my door, grab the food, and follow her up the steps to the front door.

"I usually come through the garage, I haven't used this key in forever, I hope it still works," she laughs.

I follow her inside. The foyer boasts a big space and is bigger than my bathroom. White marble flooring and beautiful hardwood furnishings adorn this space.

She walks through a large opening into the living room, another beautiful large room with maroon and teal furnishings and area rugs on top of the marble tiles. A wall-to-wall fireplace adorns the back wall.

I walk through the room and follow her into the open-concept kitchen, where a large island separates the living room from the kitchen. A small table and two chairs sit to the left in front of a large window overlooking an enormous backyard. The kitchen is a chef's dream. It's bigger than mine by quite a bit, with stainless steel appliances and cabinets from floor to ceiling. I set the food down on the island.

Emily moves to the refrigerator and retrieves a bottle of water and a bottle of wine. Then she moves to a cabinet to the left of the sink and pulls down two wine glasses, sitting them on the island near the food.

"Do you want wine or water?" She looks at me with a smile.

I laugh, "I'll take wine with the meal and water for later."

"That's what I figured you would say." She takes a corkscrew from a drawer on the island and opens the bottle of wine. Then she pours both of us a glass, sliding one toward me.

I begin to remove the food from the restaurant bag and set Emily's in front of her. "This smells delicious."

"Mmmm...yes, it does. I'm starving." She picks up her food and heads to the small table near the window.

I follow her with my food. "You have a nice place here. I love your backyard view."

She swallows her food, "Thank you. I found this place on a whim. The realtor told me about it and said it was on a short sale. The previous owners were in foreclosure, and I bought it for a song. I fell in love with the backyard." She put more food in her mouth.

I watch her chew her food slowly before taking a sip of her wine. Her eyes meet mine, and we watch each other for a brief second.

"After we finish eating, I have something to show you. I think you might like it." She smiles at me.

"Then let's hurry up and finish. I'm intrigued."

We finish our food, and I drink the rest of my wine. Standing, I pick up our trash and move to throw everything in the trash.

Emily follows me. She picks up the bottle of water from the island, looks at me, and says, "Follow me."

So, I did. We go back through the living room to a hallway off to the right. Instead of going upstairs, we go downstairs.

"Where are we going?"

She looks back at me and puts her finger to her lips. Then she wiggles her finger with the come here motion.

At the bottom of the stairs is a door. She takes a key from her pants pocket, unlocks the door, opens it, and turns to me. "Welcome to my dungeon." She moves her arm wide and smiles at me.

When I walk in, the room is filled with various 'toys.' There is a sex swing in the corner, a wall with an assortment of playthings, and a short, rounded bench.

I'm sure my mouth is on the floor.

She laughs at me, "Wanna play?" Her tongue darts out and licks her lips.

I think my face must have changed red colors several times. "I had no idea you were into this. I'm not sure what I'm doing. I've never done anything like this before."

Emily saunters over to me, puts one arm around my neck, and strokes a finger down my cheek. "I'll teach you. If you want me to." Her voice is low and sultry. Her hand moves to my shirt, she starts unbuttoning it, and she reaches up and licks my lips.

Fuck, I'm in trouble now.

"You'll need a safe word. If I do something you don't like, use the word. What's your safe word, Alex?" Her hand floats down to my jeans and moves the zipper down with one hand.

I blink a few times, "Um...I'm not sure."

"What fruit do you dislike the most?"

"Strawberries."

She looks into my eyes, "How the hell do you not like strawberries?"

I laugh, "I get hives."

"Oh, you're allergic. Gotcha. Your safe word is strawberries. If at any time you don't want to do something, say strawberries. Do you consent to having some fun with me?"

I nod my head in the affirmative.

She shakes her head from side to side, "I need to hear your words, Alex. Do you consent to having some fun with me in my dungeon?"

"Yes, I want to try whatever you deem me worthy of."

"On your knees." Her tone changes, and now she's not as *friendly*. Is that the word I'm looking for?

I kneel in front of her and look up.

She smiles, "Good boy." She moves to the wall with the toys hanging on it. She moves slowly and with precise moves. Emily takes her skirt off, exposing a pair of black silk stockings and garter belts. She removes what looks like a whip with long strings on it.

As she walks back toward me, she's not smiling anymore. Her eyes focus on mine. When she is in front of me again, she puts her leg up on a low bar I hadn't even noticed. I can smell her sex.

My dick goes hard instantly.

"Take your shirt off."

I remove my shirt and toss it to the side.

"Now your pants and boxers."

I do as she says. I'm kneeling in front of her again. When I look down between her legs, her pussy is glistening. The pantyhose has a hole just where I can see her beautiful pussy.

"You want this pussy?"

"Yes." It's all I can say. My tongue is salivating.

She moves her leg down off the bar and walks behind me. The whip hits my back, but not hard. Then she moves it along my back and hits my ass a little harder with it. She moves back in front of me, moves to a small table, then sits down with her legs spread wide.

"I think you have been a good boy. Come to me."

I start to get up.

"No! On your knees. Be a good boy and come to me." Her voice is back to the soft, sultry tone.

Moving on my knees, somehow, this does not feel as degrading as I thought it would. I get in front of her, and she stops me.

"Now, if you don't lick my pussy you'll get punished. Make me feel good."

I lean into her, attack her pussy, and devour her center like a hungry man.

"Suck my clit," she moans.

I must be doing something right. I continue licking and sucking her nub and stroking my tongue into her pussy. My God, this woman is fantastic.

She hits my back with the whip again, "Make me come."

Moving my tongue in and out of her pussy, licking up to flick her clit, I feel her walls tighten around my tongue. She's close. I suck her nub into my mouth again, and she explodes.

"Fuck yeah! Fuck." After a few seconds, she looks at me, "That's such a good boy. Back up a little so I can stand."

I move back.

"You are amazing. You did good. I'm going to get another toy, this one is for you."

I watch her pull something from the wall. It looks like a long spatula. She removes her top, exposing her voluminous breasts. She is wearing a black lacy bra, and her nipples are protruding.

I want to suck them into my mouth.

She hands me the item, "This is a riding crop. I like to be spanked. Wanna spank me, Alex?"

"Yes."

"My safe word is red. If it gets too much for me, I'll say red. I do like it hard though." Her voice is low and sexy. She turns, bends over, putting her hands on the short table, and her ass sticking up in my direction. "Stand. Spank me. I need you to spank me."

I do as I'm told. Standing, I lightly spank her with the crop.

"Harder."

The next swat is harder.

"Yes. Fuck, yes. Stick your dick in my pussy. Slam into me."

Fucking yes, I line my dick up with her center and shove it deep and hard inside her.

"Yes, fucking perfect. Good boy. Spank me."

I continue to slam my dick into her and hit her with the crop.

"Talk dirty to me. Can you do that?"

"Fucking good girl, you like my dick?"

"Yes...fuck yes..." She grips the side of the table, holding herself in place.

My dick pounds into her, my balls are hitting her clit, and I spank her again.

"Oh...yes...fuck...yes..."

I'm trying to hold myself back, but I need to come. Fucking her is the highlight of my life.

"Yes...fuck...come...come in me," she's panting.

Thank fuck! I throw the crop down, grab her hips, and pound hard and fast inside her pussy. "I'm coming...fuck..." growling out my release, I hold her hips tight to me and don't move for a few seconds.

"That was...fuck that was good." She's panting and trying to catch her breath.

I'm also trying to catch my breath. "Fuck, yeah it was."

After several seconds of breathing and calming down, my dick slides out of her wetness, and we both moan.

Emily stands up, "I totally had other intentions for tonight, but that was way better than I imagined it to be. Damn, you are good."

I smile, "I had no idea you were into this kind of stuff. I'm willing to learn more."

She laughs, "Good, I want to teach you more. Let's get cleaned up and head upstairs."

I grab my clothes, and she grabs hers. We make our way back upstairs.

I follow her to her bedroom, and we go into the bathroom ensuite.

She turns on the shower, strips out of the rest of her clothes, and steps in. "Come on in."

Again, I do as I'm told. I think I might follow this woman to the ends of the earth. Fuck, she's amazing.

We shower, dry off, and head to her bed.

She flops down, "Come on, let's rest. We'll think tomorrow. I'm tired."

I crawled beside her, pulled her into me, and we both fell asleep.

Chapter 11

Emily

With Chet safely in jail, being held without bond, I'm able to proceed with running Nordic. I know I'm not family, but the Griffins treated me like family.

Sitting at the kitchen table, I look out over the backyard. Mr. Griffin, Chet's father, helped me find this place. He and my grandfather had been friends back in the day. Chet didn't approve of his family giving me so much attention, which is one reason I broke up with him. The other is his many transgressions with other women while we were dating.

Chet's grandfather warned him that if he didn't straighten up, he would lose everything. Chet didn't believe him. Chet's father told him the same thing. Only Mr. Griffin took it one step further; he made it legal for me to own the company. I still have to report to the board of trustees, but they understand and know what Chet's father wanted.

My next move is to hire a CFO that I trust.

When I turn from my musings, Alex is standing at the opening of the kitchen, leaning up against the door frame, dressed in his normal business attire. He's a very handsome young man. And he is willing to allow me to do some of the things I like to do sexually. How far will he be willing to go before he says enough? How long before he gets tired of an older woman? I guess we'll find out.

I smiled at him, "Good morning."

Alex began to walk toward me, "Good morning. You didn't wake me."

"No, you looked so peaceful sleeping, and I didn't want to disturb that perfect look on your face." I stood, carrying my coffee cup back to the coffee maker. "Coffee?"

He moved up behind me. "Yes, please. I'd like a lot more, but I know we have to get to the office."

"You know, you're going to get a reputation around the office if we keep coming in together." I turned with a cup of coffee in my hand.

Alex kissed my nose and took the cup. "I don't care."

"You don't care that people will think you slept your way to the top?" I looked surprised.

"I'm not sleeping my way to the top. I'm perfectly satisfied staying your personal assistant." He moved toward the table and then turned, "besides, I like where I'm at and I like you."

Feeling my cheeks pinken a bit, I said, "You don't want to move up? You'd stay where you are because of me?"

He takes a sip of his coffee and glances out the window before answering. Then he turns his head my way: "I only want to move up if my skills and training afford me that. I will not be given a promotion because my girlfriend is the boss."

My eyebrows shoot up, "Girlfriend? You see me as your girlfriend?"

He laughs, "Yeah, I see you as my girlfriend. I like you, and you like me. We like to do stuff together. I get you. Why do you not want that title?"

I move toward him, he sits back in his chair, and I sit on his lap. "I didn't think you would want to be saddled with an older woman. My age doesn't bother me, but I thought it might bother you."

When he looks at me with his beautiful eyes, I almost melt. He stares into my eyes and says, "The only thing that bothers me about your age is that you keep bringing it up. We are grown-ass adults, and we can date whomever we want to. Now, do you wanna be my girlfriend or not?"

I watch his eyes for just a moment, and I know he is serious. A smile spreads across my face; I wrap my arms around his neck and nearly shout, "Yes...yes, I will be your girlfriend! We just need to be very careful at the office."

He pulls me closer to him, his lips almost on mine. "Oh, I can be very careful at the office." Then his lips are on mine, hard, fast, and needy.

Finally, pulling back from the kiss so I can breathe, I start to get up, and he won't let me. "We need to get to the office I've got to start looking for a new CFO. You have work to do, and I have work to do."

"Just give me one more minute to hold my new girlfriend." He pulls me close, wrapping his arms around my waist. I indulge him and hold him to me.

We sit like this for a few minutes, just taking in each other.

We'll see how far this goes. Men don't typically want to stay with a woman who is fifteen years older than they are and successful. Time will tell.

One week later

Alex walks into my office, stands in front of my desk, and says, "Chet's hearing has been set for December 12th."

I look at him and scoff, "That's six months from now. Are they letting him out on bond?"

"No, his bail has been denied. He's fired four lawyers since all this started. No one can get the judge to change her mind."

I laugh, "Good. Where are we on the board meeting for Monday?"

Alex chuckles, "We're good. It's after five. Let's get out of here."

For the past week, we have been going between his place and mine. I've discovered that when he is feeling overly sexual, we go to mine. He loves my sex room. He loves being told what to do. When we want more of a relaxing evening, we go to his place. It's actually been nice. I still have my doubts that this could be anything but a fling.

I remove my glasses from my face, look deep into his gorgeous eyes, and ask, "What do you have in mind?"

Alex leans down, placing his hands on the edge of my desk, leaning over, and whispers, "Pizza!"

We both break out in a loud laugh.

Then, there is a knock on my door.

"Come in."

Alex moves to the side of my desk as Malcome Newstat walks through the door.

Malcome is an up-and-coming financial whiz. He's thirty, stocky and full of himself. Malcome smiles at me and ignores Alex. "Good evening, Ms. VanZant. I was hoping to have a word with you in private." Then he glanced at Alex before returning his gaze to me. His smile is nauseating.

I clear my throat, "Good evening, Mr. Newstat. Anything you need to say to me, you can say in front of my assistant. What do you need? Is your new office adequate?"

I hesitated about hiring Malcome, but the board insisted that his qualifications were impeccable, and I needed him on my team. So, against my gut, I hired him.

He jerks his head toward Alex and then back to me. "I was hoping we could have dinner tonight and discuss some things I would like to do with the company."

"Make an appointment with Alex for next week and we can discuss those things at that time. I do not have dinner appointments regarding business. Is there anything else I can help you with?"

He scoffs, "But you'll have dinner with your assistant? Isn't that against company policy? Dating co-workers?"

I laugh, "No, it's not in the policy that we can't date co-workers. Did you actually read the policy and procedures that you signed off on?

You would know what was in there if you had. My private life is not anyone's business but mine. If you have an issue with this, you may file a grievance with the board. But I will let you know, I am the owner of this company, and I will do what I so choose. If necessary, I can replace any member of my staff company wide. I only take suggestions from the board." I stand because sitting is now not an option.

Alex comes to my side; he doesn't touch me, but he's there for support.

"I will, and always have, been a professional. My professional life and my personal life are mine and mine alone. I suggest, if you have an issue with that, you can find employment elsewhere." My blood pressure has risen considerably, and I'm not letting this punk-ass kid try to railroad me.

Malcome points his finger at me, "You will regret ever crossing me. You don't have all the power you think you have. You don't know who you are dealing with. My father is a very powerful man in this town."

I laugh, "Malcome, I have known your father for years. Mr. Griffin introduced us many years ago. You don't have as much power as you think you have. I suggest you clear out your office." I turn to Alex, "Call Ned, please."

Alex picks up my phone and proceeds to get ahold of security.

"The board hired me, not you." Malcome seems to have an illusion he has a ground to stand on.

Again, I laugh, "No, I hired you on their recommendation and against my better judgment. So, now, I'm firing you. You may meet my security team in your office and vacate the premises within one hour. Good day." I move around my desk as Alex hangs up the phone.

"They will meet you in your office. I suggest you do as Ms. VanZant has said and vacate the building." Alex moves next to me.

I wave my arm out, showing Malcome to the door. "This way out, Mr. Newstat."

You can tell Malcome is furious; his face is six shades of red. He storms out of my office and down the long hallway to his office.

The rest of the staff is gone for the day, and the building is relatively quiet. The elevator dings, and three security officers step off. I say hello to each of them, and they head to the CFO's office.

Looking over at Alex, I say, "Let's go get some pizza."

We laugh all the way to the car.

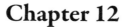

Chapter 12

Alex

Well, that was fun to watch. I loved seeing Emily on fire. She really knows how to handle tough situations, and that asshole deserves everything he gets.

As we get into her BMW, I look over at her, "That was awesome."

She smiles, "I hate firing people. But that asshole had it coming. I will have to be more careful about who I hire. I should have listened to my gut."

"Always go with your gut. If it's a bad choice, then you can only blame yourself. But usually, your gut will tell you the move to make and it's usually correct." I put my hand on hers, which is resting on the gearshift between us. "You did great. I'll start looking for his replacement on Monday."

"Check with Ashley over at the college. She might have an idea of what's out there as far as financial leaders." She shifts the car into gear, and we head to my house.

On nights like tonight, I like to go to my place. It's low-key, and we can relax. I truly love going to Emily's house, and our sex life is fantastic. I have the best of both worlds: low-key when we need a relaxing night and dark, wild, out-of-this-world fantastic when we want more. She's an enigma. She's light and dark.

I pull my phone out of my pocket and open the pizza app, ordering the large supreme thick-crust pizza, two salads, and breadsticks—our normal.

Emily makes her way across town to my apartment. When she pulls into the spot, she has designated it as 'hers.' She looks over at me and says, "You don't think I did anything wrong with Malcome, do you?"

I shake my head, "No, you did exactly what you should have done. He's a prick. I'm glad he's gone."

She nods, "I agree. Okay, I just wanted to make sure I didn't do anything wrong. I'll call Todd in a bit to let him know what went down."

"I texted him on our way here. He's expecting your call later this evening." I put my phone back in my pocket, get out of the car, and head to her side.

When I open her door, she smiles. "Thank you. You are always a gentleman." She clicks her key fob as we walk into the building.

We say hello to the doorman, get on the elevator, and as soon as the doors close, Emily launches herself at me. Her lips are burning with desire, kissing up and down my neck, finding my lips, her tongue thrusts into my mouth. Our tongues fight for dominance. Her legs are wrapped around my waist, and we push against the back wall of the elevator, hands, tongues, and arms finding places to pinch, slap, and kiss.

The elevator makes its dinging noise, letting us know that we are on my floor. As fast as she jumped me, she is back to her normal self, standing next to me. We are both panting a little, but fuck, that was hot. The doors open, and we move to the exit, holding hands.

We laugh at our antics and the way we attacked each other just a minute before. God, she's perfect.

When I open the door to the apartment, she enters and begins taking off her shoes and skirt and unbuttoning her blouse.

"What are you doing? The pizza will be here shortly. We don't have time..." I didn't finish.

She is on her knees in front of me, undoing my belt and zipper and pulling them down to the ground. Emily watches my eyes as she moves closer. Her tongue darts out and licks the pre-cum already forming on the tip of my dick.

"Fuck!" That is all I can say.

Her mouth slides down the shaft of my cock, so slowly I think I might come before she makes it to the base. As she moves up and down my shaft with her hot wet mouth, her tongue does some crazy shit around the tip before she sucks me back down her throat. Then, she moans.

My dick vibrates. "Fuck, Em, I'm going to come. Fuck!"

Mmmmmm...more vibrations.

I grab her head, tangle my fingers in her hair, and fuck her mouth until I shoot cum all down her throat. "Fuck...fuck...fffuuuccckkk!!!"

As she pulls off my cock, licks the last bit of cum from her lips, she swallows. The smile of satisfaction on her face is enough to make me want to fuck her pussy.

"Damn, woman, that was fantastic. Fuck, what got into you?" I begin to pull my pants up and zip them.

She laughs, "I felt like you needed a release, so, I gave you one. I'll be right back." She disappears down the hallway and into the bathroom.

The intercom rings, and I answer it. "Yes."

"Your delivery has arrived sir. I'll send Tony right up with it. Do you need anything further tonight?" The concierge for my building is Mack. He's a tough ass dude.

"Thank you Mack, that will be it. I appreciate you." I'll have to remember to give him a special gift in the next week or so. He has really stepped up his game since Emily and I have been coming to my place. He never judges.

After a few minutes, there is a knock on the door, and I open it. Tony, the building's bellman, is standing there with a table on rollers and all of our food, which we ordered from the pizza place.

"Thank you, Tony. Just put it over there." I point to the side of the door. We can move it later. I passed Tony a ten-dollar bill. "I appreciate you bringing that up."

"No problem sir, if you need anything else, just ring down."

"I will."

Tony left just as Emily emerged from the bathroom. "Oh my gosh, that smells delicious. I'm starving." She heads for the table with the food on it.

"I thought I just filled you up." I smiled a big toothy grin.

She laughed, "Oh, you did. But I need sustenance. And the smell is killing me. My stomach is doing flip flops."

I get two plates, hand her one, and we dig in. The pizza, salad, and breadsticks were just what we needed to finish the night off.

What a fucking day…here's hoping tomorrow is less eventful.

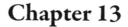

Chapter 13

Emily

The next morning, I'm working in my office and my private line rings. I stare at it. No one but a handful of people knows that number. Two are dead, and one is in jail. The other three shouldn't have a reason to call me: the president of the board, Todd Triplett, Mr. Tollman, the retired CFO that I took his place, and my mother. She never calls, so it can't be her.

After it rang for the third time, I finally picked it up. "Hello."

"Emily, James Tollman. I'm sorry to bother you. I've just returned from a long vacation with my wife and heard about all the things that have happened there. Do you need my help?"

I let out the breath I was holding, "Oh sir, thank you for the offer but I think I have it under control now. I hired a CFO to replace me but found out that he was not good for the company. I'm in the market for another CFO. Other than that, things have been running rather smoothly since Chet went to jail."

He let out a huff, "That asshole. I'm glad he's getting what was coming to him. I'll send over a list of a few CFOs that I've had some dealings with that are reputable. Maybe one of them will work for you."

"That would be much appreciated sir. Thank you so much. I do want to say, you are missed around here." I smile into the phone.

"Well, I would say I missed the hustle and bustle but to be honest, I'm really enjoying retirement." He laughs, "If you need any help at all, you call me. I'll send that list over through your email."

"I appreciate it sir. Thank you very much. Much love to your wife and enjoy those grandkids."

He laughs, "Will do. Talk to you later."

We hang up the phone. That isn't as bad as I thought it would be. I hate getting calls on that private number. It means that the call doesn't go through the switchboard downstairs and can't be traced as easily.

The day seems to be going by quite quickly. I look at my watch, and it is already three in the afternoon. I've been working nonstop most of the day.

There is a slight knock on my door, and Alex's head pops around the corner. "Hey, you haven't taken a break all day. Are you starving? I can run and get us some food."

I smile at him, "No, I'm fine. I think we can have an early dinner if that's okay with you, unless you have other plans."

He walks into my office, puts his hands on the edge of my desk, and says, " Why would I have any other plans? I have spent the last month with you. Why would that change?"

I shrug, "Alex we never really even talked about our relationship. I don't want you to feel like you're being pushed into this."

Alex stands straight up, walks around my desk, and takes my hands in his. He pulls me from my chair, looks me in the eye, and expresses his feelings. "Never once have I ever felt that I was being pushed into this relationship. Never once have I complained about this relationship. If you don't want to be in a relationship with me you need to let me know. Because right now I can't see myself without you. Emily Van Zant, I think I'm falling for you pretty damn hard."

I take a deep breath, and I look down at our clasped hands, then back up into his eyes. "Alex, thank you, I think I just needed to hear that. I never want you to feel like you were pushed into this relationship with me. I know I'm older than you and that has got to mean something to you. I'm not just a few years older, I'm fifteen years older. What will your family say? Your friends? I just don't want you to regret anything."

He squeezes my hands, brings me into him, wraps his arms around me, and kisses the tip of my nose. When he looks into my eyes again, he says, "I don't give a fuck about what anyone says. I'm in love with you. My family and friends will understand. If they don't, fuck them. This is between you and me. The only way out of this, would be if you leave me."

For the first time in a long time, I think a tear falls from my eyes and slides down my cheek. No one in my life has ever said such beautiful words. "You love me?" I do one of those giggle cries.

He smiles back at me, "Yes, Emily, I'm in love with you, heart and soul. I know it hasn't been very long, but like I said I cannot see myself without you."

His lips touch mine softly. Not demanding, not needy, but as a man in love.

As we pull back from the kiss, I look into his beautiful brown eyes and say, "I love you too."

This time, his lips are on mine, hard, fast, and needy.

Unfortunately, we are interrupted by the phone ringing. When I look, it is my private line again. Surely, Mr. Tollman hasn't found someone for me already. He said he was sending over the list by e-mail. Maybe he forgot my e-mail address. I pick up the phone, almost laughing, "Mr. Tollman, did you forget my e-mail address?"

"No sweetheart, what I need must be done in person." Chet's voice comes over the line.

I pull the receiver from my ear and stare at it briefly. Then, I stare into Alex's eyes. "What do you want, Chet?"

Chapter 14

Alex

I step back from Emily slightly, giving her a strange look. She leans over her desk, grabs a pen and a piece of paper, and starts scribbling something.

She hands it to me.

Get Ned to call the police; Chet has gone crazy.

I nod and run out to my office. I get Ned on the phone. "Chet is on Emily's private line. Get the police here ASAP!" I hang up the phone and run back into Emily's office.

I mouth to her, "Put it on speaker."

Her hands are visibly shaking as she moves to put the phone on speaker.

I hear Chet's disgusting voice on the other end. "If you do exactly as I say no one will get hurt."

"I thought you were in jail. What happened? How did you get out?" Emily's voice is steady, but her hands are shaky. She falls into her chair. "What do you want to chat about?"

Chet chuckles, "Several things, actually. I want my bank account restored. I want the private jet fueled at the airport, ready to go. And you must be on the plane."

Emily scoffs, "You must be insane. There's no way I'm going with you anywhere. Where the hell do you think you're going? And how did you get out of jail?"

He laughs again. "My lawyer found a loophole. I was released about an hour and a half ago. And you will do what I say or completely lose the company altogether."

Emily looked at me before she spoke.

I scribbled on a piece of paper.

Police are on the way.

She nodded her head. "What kind of loophole?"

Chet is getting impatient. "Shut up bitch. Doesn't matter. I'm out of here. That's all that matters. Now bank account, jet, and you at the airport in two hours."

"I am not going with you anywhere. I can't unfreeze your bank accounts, that was not me. And you're not taking the plane anywhere." Emily is getting her composure back, and now she is getting mad.

Chet chuckles wildly. "I thought you might say that at the beginning, so let me tell you what's going on. If my demands are not met, I'll just blow up the fucking building."

Emily's eyes grow as big as saucers when she looks at me. She stares at me as she says the next words. "You are trying to threaten me with a bomb. No fucking way."

Chet appears in the office, turns off his cell, and moves toward Emily and me in slow motion, opening his jacket to expose something strapped to his chest: a bomb. "I'll detonate this motherfucker if you don't do as I say."

I move slowly to my desk. There is an emergency button on the inside panel. If I can make it, the police will be here soon. I move so slowly no one sees me move. Hopefully, Chet won't notice.

I look at Emily and give her a keep-talking movement with my finger. She's got to keep Chet talking and focusing on her. "Chet, you can't blow up this building. Your grandfather built this company. You don't want to do that."

"Watch me bitch! I'm sick of your shit. Now, pick up the phone, get Ned, tell him what I want and if I see cops, this building comes down." Chet's eyes looked crazy. Wild, like he's on something.

"Chet..." Emily kept trying to talk to him.

"Shut...the...fuck...up!" He screamed.

I saw Emily shake slightly. "Fine. I'll call Ned." She picked up the phone and hit Ned's number.

"Ms. VanZant, what can I do for you?" Ned answered.

"I need several things. Chet is in my office with a bomb strapped to his chest. He is demanding that his bank account restored, a jet, and me to accompany him. He says no police, or he blows up the building. Make it happen, now." She never let her eyes leave Chet's.

I give her a slight nod, letting her know I've pushed the button on my desk.

"Ms. VanZant, I will do what you need me to. Know that the police are on their way..."

Chet yells, "put him on speaker. I don't trust you."

She moves her hand to the phone and pushes the speaker. " You are now on speaker, Ned. Please do as he says so we can get out of this alive."

Chet smiled his nasty ass smile.

Ned answered, "Yes ma'am. How much money do you need Mr. Griffin?"

"One...no two million. Small bills. That will hold me until my accounts are restored. Fueled jet at the private strip. Meet me in the garage in thirty minutes."

Ned said, "I can't get the money that fast. Give me at least a couple of hours."

"Thirty minutes, asshole. That's all you have." Chet is starting to sweat.

"Do the best you can, Ned. Call my bank, tell them what we need, and they will do it." Emily is remaining as calm as she can during this whole thing.

"Yes ma'am." Ned hung up the phone.

Emily looked at Chet, "Happy? You will get what you want. Now, can you defuse the bomb? Please. Don't hurt innocent people."

Chet laughs, "It will be your fault if anyone gets hurt. You are the one that is making my life hell. You are the one that stole my company. You are the one that somehow got my father to sign over my birthright. It's all your fault."

I think he finally remembered that I was there and turned abruptly. "Asshole, get over here. You'll be the first to die."

I move over to where Emily is, behind her desk. I move between the desk and her in a protective stance. "You will not get away with this. If you blow up anything, you will blow yourself up. You don't want to die. You want to live. You want that money. Take the money and go wherever you want. No one will follow you."

Chet laughs out loud, hard, and nearly doubles over. "You think you can talk your way out of anything, don't you pretty boy. I'm not going anywhere without that bitch behind you. She's going to pay for what she's done to me."

Chet starts pacing around the room. It had been almost fifteen minutes since Emily talked to Ned. He's walking over by the window. Shit!

Emily notices, too. She gets his attention. "Chet, why are you doing this? This is what your father wanted. He didn't want his company to go under. That's where it was heading."

Chet starts moving toward me, "You, bitch, are the reason I'm doing this. My father would have never given this company away had you not persuaded him to do so. This is my fucking company!" he started screaming and ranting incoherently.

Another fifteen minutes go by. Her phone finally rings.

I look at Chet, "It may be Ned."

"Answer it!" Chet screams at Emily.

She picks up the phone. Ned's voice is on the other end. "Ms. VanZant, I have everything in place. All of your requests. What do you want me to do next?"

She looks at Chet, "What now? He has everything ready."

Chet smiles dementedly, "Meet us downstairs in the garage. We'll take your car."

"Did you hear that, Ned?" She asks.

"Yes ma'am. We'll have the money in the trunk of your car. The plane is at the private airstrip. Everything is in place."

I take what Ned is saying, as the police would be in place as well. I'm hoping anyway.

Emily looked at me, "I'll be fine. Ned has assured me that everything is ready and in place."

"I can't let you go with this asshole. He's delusional." I stepped in front of her with a worried look on my face.

"I'll be fine. Let me go. Everything will be fine." She put her hand on my chest, "I'll be back."

"The fuck you will, you will never see this place again, bitch," Chet spouted off.

Emily mouthed to me, 'I'll be fine. Police are downstairs.'

I leaned down and kissed her.

"Awe, how cute. Let's go bitch."

Emily stepped back from me, "I'll be fine." She walked toward Chet.

Chet grabbed her arm, pulled her toward the door of the office, and then pulled her out to the elevator. He dragged her onto the elevator, pushed the G on the panel, and the elevator started to descend.

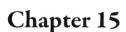

Chapter 15

Emily

"Chet, this is not necessary. Just let me go. We'll figure something out." I'm trying to get free from this psycho.

Chet just laughs, "You will not figure out something. You took everything from me bitch, everything. My family business, my home, my name, my life...you fucking took it all."

"Chet, I only took the company. It was your father's wishes, not mine. I only did what he wanted done." I try like hell to explain that it wasn't me.

He looks up at the ceiling of the elevator, then blows out a breath. "My attorney told me that I had nothing. Everything was wrapped up in the company. I didn't even have a home to go back to when I got out of jail. You took it all."

I look at him with surprise. "No, I only had the deed to the company. What are you talking about?"

He shakes his head, "Dad put everything in the company name. Therefore, my lovely ex, you acquired my family home, all the money, the company, everything. Every-fucking-thing. You fucked me out of my inheritance. But guess what? You aren't going to be around to see any of it. You are going to be my ticket out of here and I will make you suffer for the rest of your miserable life for what you've done to me." He pokes the gun I didn't even know he had in my side.

My eyes go to the red light on the bomb. He is currently holstering around his midsection. "Chet, you won't get away with this. The police are going to find you and you will go to jail for the rest of your life. Do you want that?"

"Oh no, sweetheart, I'm getting out of here with you in tow. You are going to be my ticket out of this fucking place. I'll take my money and start over. But you, you will suffer for the rest of your life."

The elevator opens in the garage. When we step out, I look around, hoping to see some police or something, nothing. I see nothing or no one. The garage is empty. The cars that were here earlier are gone. At least they got most of the people out of the building. My BMW is sitting there in its normal spot.

Where are the police? Surely they aren't going to let me go with this asshole. What the fuck?

Chet pushes me toward my car, "Get in."

"Chet, I don't have my keys. I can't go anywhere." I try to explain.

He narrows his eyes at me, "You have a spare set under the seat, remember...I know you."

Fuck! I was hoping he wouldn't remember that. "They aren't there. I moved them after we broke up. I gave the spare set to Alex." Hopefully, he'll buy that story.

"Why the fuck would you do that? Pretty boy doesn't need to drive a fucking BMW. Come on...we will take my car." He pulls me toward the street entrance.

As we get to the open door that leads out to the street entrance, he pokes the gun into my side again. "Put the code in. I know you have changed that as well."

"Chet, really, let's talk about this."

He screams, spittle flying out of his mouth, "Shut...the...fuck...up...bitch! Code...now!"

My hand is shaking badly. I start to put the code in and there is a loud noise behind us.

When Chet turns, he loses his grip on my arm, and I toss myself to the side behind a concrete pillar.

Shots ring out, echoing throughout the entire underground garage. I watch Chet's body fall to the ground. In seconds, there are several officers in what look like spacesuits swarming around Chet's lifeless body. A man is kneeling next to me, saying something.

I couldn't take my eyes off Chet's body. He's just lying there while the people surrounding him are working on the bomb.

Tears stream down my face.

"Ma'am? Are you hurt? Ma'am...can you hear me?"

I look up, and several police officers are staring at me. Then, I hear my name.

"Emily...Emily...God, are you alright?"

I look around to see where the voices are coming from. Alex is running toward me. He fought through a couple of officers and fell to his knees in front of me. "God, are you alright? Did you get hurt?" He's running his hands through my hair, over my body, like he's making sure I'm still alive.

I find his eyes, "I'm fine," I choke out in a low voice.

He pulls me into him, holding me close to his chest. "Thank God! I was so worried. They wouldn't let me through. I finally just...it doesn't matter, I'm here. What do you need?"

My arms wrap around his waist, holding him to me. He was my lifeline. He was my safe space. "Just to get out of here."

Alex gently pulls away slightly, "Okay, let me see what we need to do." He doesn't let go of me but turns to find an officer standing close by. "Hey, she needs to get somewhere away from here. Where can we go?"

I hear him talking but never hear anything else.

Alex starts pulling me to my feet, still not letting me go, and we make our way back toward the same elevator that I just got off.

I glance back to see Chet's lifeless body lying on the cement ground, blood pooling around his head. Someone lays a cloth over his body, but his face is still visible. His eyes are still open, looking up, his mouth slightly open; he looks shocked. Then, I bury my face in Alex's side.

Alex gets us on the elevator, hits the button for the top floor, and we head back to my office.

"Alex, what...what happened?" I stammer out the question.

His arm tightens around my shoulders, "I'll explain everything when we get upstairs." He pulls out his phone, hits a button, then starts talking into it. "Get me some coffee, dry toast, and water sent up to Ms. VanZant's office now." Then, he hangs up the phone.

"Who...who was that?" I can't seem to get my mouth to speak correctly.

"The deli next door. They have some things sent over that will not upset your stomach, but we need to get something in you before you pass out."

The elevator doors open; we walk slowly toward my office and shut the door when we enter.

Alex moves me toward the sofa in the corner of my office that I never use. We sit down together, and he holds me to him.

That's when the waterworks start. The tears start falling down my cheeks, and I have no control over them. My body is shaking. I can't get it to stop.

Alex pulls a small blanket from the back of the sofa. I'm glad I put that there. He wraps it around me, and then he just holds me for a long time, allowing me cry.

I can't help all the tears. I have no idea why I am crying. I don't care about Chet, and I don't care about what he did. So, why all the tears? What is my body doing to me?

There is a knock at the door, and Alex says come in. He is not leaving my side.

Ned walks in with a white paper bag, a large thermos, and several bottles of water. He sits them down on the coffee table in front of the sofa. He addresses Alex, "How is she?"

"She'll be fine. She's in shock. The tears have subsided some. But she'll be fine. How are things going downstairs?" Alex is sitting forward, his leg touching mine, as he prepares the coffee and takes out the toast from the bag. He hands me a slice of dry toast. "Here, eat some of this."

I swipe at the tears on my cheeks, take the toast, and bite a small bite.

He hands me the cup of coffee, just like I like it, with cream and sugar. "Sip on this. It's hot, but it will help." He turns back to Ned. "Can you get a warm wash cloth from the bathroom, please?"

After a few minutes, I feel the warm cloth touch my face, and I look up to see Alex dabbing it on my cheeks. The pain in his eyes is heartbreaking.

I reach up and put my hand on his cheek. "I'm going to be okay. I just needed to get out of that garage."

Ned speaks, "Ms. VanZant, the employees have been told to go home for the day. What do you need me to do?"

"Shut everything down until Monday. We will regroup and start fresh next week. I need to give a press conference as soon as possible. We don't want anyone getting the wrong impression of our company." I think my brain is finally catching up to my thoughts.

"Yes ma'am. I'll let everyone know. I'll have Sue get the press conference set up. When do you want to do it?" Ned asks.

"As soon as possible. This is going to be newsworthy, and I want to make sure things don't get misunderstood. Within the next hour or so. I'll get myself together." I explain in more detail than necessary.

"Yes ma'am," Ned leaves the office.

I look into Alex's eyes, "thank you for taking care of me. I don't know what I would have done if you hadn't been there. I think I'm better now. Can you be by my side for the press conference?"

He smiles, "I wouldn't be anywhere else."

I finish the toast and coffee, then make my way to the bathroom, where I can get myself put back together. What a hell of a day it's been so far. I need to go home and go to bed.

When I come out of the bathroom, Alex looks at me and says, "The police need a statement as soon as you can. They want to talk to both of us."

I nod, "Not before the press conference. They can wait."

My desk phone rings, and I answer it.

"Ms. VanZant," Ned's voice comes over the line." The press conference is set for two p.m. this afternoon."

"Thank you, Ned." I hang up and tell Alex.

Will this day ever end?

Chapter 16

Emily

I have never been so scared in my entire life. I had to wash the blood from my face—Chet's blood. I'll get through this. I know I will. It's just going to take me a hot minute. I have to face the press in less than an hour. Alex has not left my side. This is just a fucked-up day.

After I clean up and change my clothes, I return to my office, where Alex is waiting. "Hey, thank you for being here with me. You have no idea how much this means to me." I move to sit back down on the sofa where I was earlier.

Alex moves to sit next to me. "I wouldn't be anywhere else. I'll be right by your side during the press conference. Do you know what you're gonna say?"

I let out a long breath. "I think so. Basically, that we had a bomber and it's been taken care of. No one was hurt from the company and the police acted quickly in this story. I just really want everyone to know that everything is OK here."

Alex watches me for a few minutes. Then he softly speaks. "I agree. I believe you need to make sure that the company is taken care of, the employees were sent home in a timely manner, and the threat was subdued quickly by law enforcement."

I look over at him and smile. "Maybe you should give the press conference because that was good."

We both laugh. It feels good to laugh for once today.

There's a knock on my door, and I say come in.

Ned walks through the door and says, "Ms. VanZandt, the press conference is ready and set up. They're ready whenever you are."

"Thank you, Ned, I'll be right down." I stand from the sofa.

Alex is with me. He takes my hand in his, brings it to his lips, and kisses the back of it. "I'm right by your side. Draw on my strength."

I smile, "You have to be one of the sweetest men I've ever met. Thank you. Thank you for being by my side. Most men would have run for the hills by now."

He laughs, "I'm not going anywhere sweetheart. You're stuck with me."

I inhale a deep breath and let it out slowly. "Then let's get this done."

We walk silently to the elevator, not speaking until we reach the lobby. There is a small podium, many microphones, and many media people.

Alex leans over, "You got this."

I take another small breath and head to the podium. I step up to the microphones, and the reporters all start asking questions.

Alex steps up next to me, "She will only be giving a statement today. Please, no questions."

I give him a soft smile of thanks. Then, I turn back to the crowd. "Thank you all for coming today. I appreciate your patience. I'm going to give you the facts as I know them. There is an ongoing investigation that I cannot give any information about at this time. I will do my best to give you all of the information I can. Several months ago, it came to my attention that the CEO, Chet Griffin, was misappropriating funds. Mr. Griffin was relieved of his post at that time. After further investigation into the misappropriating funds issue Mr. Griffin was arrested. That is the ongoing investigation. This morning, Mr. Griffin appeared in my office with a bomb strapped to his chest."

Gasps ring out through the crowd.

"Mr. Griffin was subdued in the basement of this building without further incident. The company is in good standing and is running effectively. The employees were sent home until Monday morning. The company will continue to run according to our by-laws. I want to thank you all again for coming out today." I start to move away from the podium.

A reporter shouts, "Is it true that he took you hostage today?"

"I cannot confirm or deny that theory. Thank you again." I step away from the podium, and Alex almost catches me in his arms.

We move back to the elevator and got back on, hitting the button for the floor where our offices are.

Ned is right by my side. "You did a great job Ms. VanZant. Well-spoken and you told the truth. That's all you can do."

"Thank you Ned, please take the rest of the afternoon off. You deserve it." I let out a sigh.

He nods, as Alex and I get off the elevator to the top floor. "I'll see you in the morning then."

Alex takes my arm and escorts me back to my office.

When we get in the room, he closes the door, and I collapse onto the sofa, and tears fall freely. This has been a fucking messed up day. I need a break from this place.

Alex sits down next to me and puts his arm around my shoulders, pulling me into him.

After several minutes of sitting like this, I finally decide to say something. "Alex, get me out of here, please."

Alex stands and pulls me up with him. "Get your purse keys and let's go."

I smile, "Thank you."

As he pulls me into him, I relax and rest my head on his chest. "Emily, I would do anything for you."

I move from his warm arms to my desk, retrieve my purse and keys, and turn back to him. "Let's go."

The elevator doors open just as we approach. We look at each other and back at the elevator. No one is there. We get on the elevator, Alex has his arm around my waist, and we go to the garage one more time today.

I am reluctant to look around the garage because I just know I will see the evidence of where Chet took his last breath. As we approach my car, I glance over to where Chet was lying just a few hours ago, with blood everywhere. Now, it's as if he was never there. No blood. No sign that anything had happened down here just a few short hours before. Erased from existence.

Alex takes my keys from me as we approach the car. He opens my door and closes it.

I settle in my seat and buckle up as he gets in the driver's seat. I look over at him. "How did they get it cleaned up so fast?"

Alex shrugs, "As soon as the police gave the OK, Ned had a crew down here getting it cleaned up. He didn't want you to have to go through anymore trauma today."

I half-smile, "Remind me to give him extra in his Christmas bonus this year."

Alex chuckles, "I'll do that." He starts the car, and we back out of my parking spot. As he drives toward the garage's exit, I lean my head back on the seat and close my eyes.

For the first time today, I am able to relax.

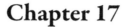

Chapter 17

Alex

It's been a week since Chet's demise and things seem to be running quite smoothly. Emily is back to her old self to a certain degree. I'm not sure anyone gets back to themselves after being held captive and having someone shot right next to them. After the incident, she had nightmares for a few nights, but she seems to be doing much better now.

I watch her closely to ensure she doesn't experience any residual backlash from what Chet did. Her employees, her company, and the board seem to be sticking by her no matter what. They have all given her the support she needs to make it through this terrible ordeal.

We've been staying at my place this week because it's low-key. Emily said she felt safer at my place than she did at hers. I'm not sure why. She lives in a gated community with security. The threat is over, but I will do whatever she wants me to do make her feel comfortable.

We're nearing the end of the day on Friday, and I step into her office. "Hey, what do you wanna do for dinner tonight?"

She looks up at me and smiles, "You."

I laugh, "Ohh really. Don't you think you might need some food? You might need to keep your strength up." I walk toward her desk.

She stands from her chair, walks around her desk, and meets me halfway in the middle of the office. "You first, food later." Her arms snake up around my neck, pulling me down to her. Our lips are just barely a whisper apart.

Of course, my dick goes hard instantly. We haven't had sex in over a week. I am not going to push her. Now, it seems that she's back to normal. I lock the door and move to her quickly.

She whispers, "My pussy is throbbing. I need to feel you inside me."

"And I want to please you, Princess." I reach between us and unbuckle my pants, unzipping them and freeing my dick.

She lifts her skirt, turns with her back toward me, leans over the desk, and sticks her ass in the air. She looks over her shoulder and smiles. "It's all yours. Take what you want."

I move up behind her, run my hand across her ass, and slap her butt cheek.

She screeches.

I slap her again, only on the other butt cheek. I rub my dick between her ass cheeks. Then reach a hand around in front of her, fingering her clit. "Are you wet for me?"

"So wet," she barely whispers.

I smile, "Good girl. Before I fuck you, you're gonna come. Come for me baby." I continue my manipulations on her clit, rubbing, pinching, and pressing down hard. "Come for me baby."

She screams, "Ohh fuck yeah."

"That's it, baby, that's it, come for me." My fingers continue to move over her hard nub.

She screams again, and her release is beautiful.

I shove my dick in her so hard she whimpers. Both my hands grab her hips, and I pound into her hard and fast. I can't help myself. It's been over a week since I fucked this pretty pussy. "God, I love your pussy, it's so amazing. You take my dick so well. Fuck yeah. Come with me. I'm coming, come with me you hear me, you fucking come with me."

After pounding hard into her for several minutes, we both let out a growling sound. I shoot my cum inside her and feel her pussy walls clench around my dick as her release comes at the same time as mine.

"Good girl, God, you're such a good girl." Neither one of us moves, my hands still on her hips; I'm still buried deep inside her.

We both are panting for air.

As our breathing evens out and we both start coming down from the most erotic high I'd ever been on, my dick slips from her wetness. We both groan from the loss.

She is still leaning over her desk, not moving. I can see cum running down her legs. I tuck my dick back into my pants, move to the bathroom to retrieve a warm wet washcloth, return, and she is still in the same position I left her. I begin wiping up her legs, between her thighs, cleaning her up, and making sure she is taken care of.

She finally stands, pulls her skirt down, and turns toward me. "That was fucking amazing, thank you." She smiles, "Now, I'm starving for food."

We both laugh out loud.

I look at her, "Then let's get some food. You wanna go to your place or mine?"

She gives me a devilish smile, "Mine."

I chuckle, "Absolutely."

This is going to be a hell of a weekend.

After two days of non-stop sex, we finally fell asleep on her large king-sized bed Saturday night, wrapped in each other's arms. Sex with Emily is the best sex I've ever had. She is so erotic and wants to be dominating but loves it when I am. She wants to be in charge, but then she loves to be submissive. It's the best of both worlds with her.

I woke up Sunday morning to her warm mouth on my dick. My eyes blink open, and my hands go to her hair as she moves her mouth up and down my shaft with perfection. My hips move up to meet her strokes. I fuck her mouth, but before I come, I pull her up to me. "I want to be buried deep in that fucking pussy of yours."

She smiles, straddles my waist, and sinks her sweet pussy down on my cock.

We both moan.

"Fuck, that feels so good. Your pussy is so fucking hot and wet." I watch her eyes as she rides my dick. They turn so dark when she is getting off.

She bounces up and down on my dick, and her boobs bounce up and down. What a beautiful sight that is.

I grab two handfuls of boobs, twisting her nipples as she pounds down on my cock.

Her voice comes out gravely, "Fuck, your dick is so good. I'm coming, fuck yes! Fffuuuccckkk!"

"Yes, come all over my dick, baby. Fuck, yes!" I feel her juices pour over my dick and drip down to my balls. Fuck, she's amazing.

I can't stand it anymore. I grab her waist, hold her still, and piston up into her sweet, wet essence. "Fuck, babe, I'm...fuck...yes...coming." I let go, and my release pounds inside her.

Emily's face goes still, her eyes roll back, and she comes with me. She's amazing. I never knew a woman could come so many times. A couple? Yes...five or six...no. She let out a breath, gripping my chest, and threw her head back, revealing in the euphoric moment.

My head is swarming with wonderful thoughts as I hold her still. I can't help the fact that this woman has turned my world upside down in such a short time.

She falls on top of me.

My hands go to her hair, and my fingers intertwine with the strands of her beautiful blonde hair. We stay this way for several long minutes.

She finally looks at me. "I have something I need to say. Don't interrupt me or I will not make it through."

I nod, "Okay."

She takes a slow, deep, cleansing breath and lets it out. "I think I'm in love with you." Her face nearly goes white.

Smiling at her, all I can say is, "I know I'm in love with you. Can you handle being with a much younger man?"

She laughs, "If you can handle being with a much older woman."

I move fast, flipping her over, and now I'm on top of her. "I can handle anything you can." I kiss her slowly, roaming my tongue over hers, searching every inch of her mouth and memorizing this moment so that I will remember it for all time. The first time we said I love you, right here, in her big bed, after having mind-blowing sex. Yes, this woman is for me.

Fuck, I'm a lucky man.

Chapter 18

Emily

I can't remember when I'd had a better weekend. Waking up, having non-stop sex, and eating. Then, do it all over again and end the weekend with each of us proclaiming our love for each other. When does that happen? Never!

Monday morning came way too soon for me. I want so badly to go back and do the weekend all over again. After last week, we deserve another day off. Unfortunately, we can't. I have to interview the next CFO. Hopefully, this one will do a better job than the last one.

Brandon Streeter walks into my office, shakes my hand, and looks accomplished.

"Mr. Streeter, it's good to meet you. I've heard some very good things about you. Have a seat," I gesture to the chair in front of my desk.

He smiles, "Thank you and I've heard some great things about you and this company."

"I'll get right to the point. I need someone that is going to get the job done without being a prick. I was the former CFO before moving to CEO. The last man I hired was not a good fit. Tell me why you would be a good fit for my company." I sit back in my chair, fold my hands over my stomach, and wait.

He clears his throat. "Ms. VanZant, Nordicis one of the up-and-coming software companies in the country. You have brought it to levels that no one else could have. I want only the best for the company and will look out for its best interests. If I see something that is not right, I will report it to you and the board. Nordic Software has an A+ rating, and I want to keep it that way."

"Why did you leave..." I pause and glance at his resume, "Murdock Financial?"

He looks down for a brief moment, collecting his thoughts. "To be honest, they were not doing things on the up and up. I will not do anything dishonest or illegal for any company."

I lean forward, arms on my desk, and question him. "They wanted you to do something illegal?"

"Not necessarily, illegal, but not moral. I refused and they said I was not working out. I want to be upfront with you, I will not do anything that is against my morals." He crosses his ankle over his knee.

Sitting back in my chair again, I nod. "I appreciate that. I would never ask you to. This company is a top-notch company. I will not tolerate going behind my back to the board or anyone else. If you have a problem, bring it to me. Make all appointments through my assistant, Mr. Bennett. I do not do dinner appointments, my time is reserved after hours for my private life. I do not expect anyone on my staff to work over. If you have an issue, it can wait until the next day. At 5:00 p.m. every day, we shut this building down. I have twenty-four-hour security, there is a day staff and a night staff as well as cameras. You are to leave the building when everyone else does at 5:00 daily. You need your personal time as much as the rest of us. Do you have any questions for me?"

"What is the benefit's package?"

"Two weeks paid vacation after one year, 401(k)-the company matches your input, ten sick days every six months. There are some other perks for working here, and human resources will go over everything when you are hired. Does this sound like something you would be interested in?"

"Yes, ma'am."

"Do you have an issue working for a woman?" I lean forward again, watching his eyes.

He never moves his eyes from mine. "No ma'am. I look up to women who make their own way."

I study his face for several minutes. He never looks away. I watch him closely before speaking again. "Mr. Streeter, welcome to Nordic Software. Can you start tomorrow?" I stand and put my hand out.

He follows my actions and shakes my hand. "Yes ma'am and I look forward to working with you."

"I'll have Alex make an appointment for you in the morning with HR. Be here at 8:00 in the morning and we will get started." I move around my desk and walk him to the door.

"Thank you again, Ms. VanZant."

I open the door, "Thank you, Mr. Streeter. See you in the morning."

He leaves my office.

I look at Alex, "Make an appointment for Brandon Streeter with HR first thing tomorrow. What's for dinner tonight? I'm starving. It's been a long day."

He laughs, "Yes it has. Let's get Chinese. My place or yours?"

I smile, "Yours, I need a break."

He comes up to me, standing close, "I didn't think you would ever need a break. You are superwoman."

I laugh, "No, I'm old. Let's have a chill night. After this weekend, I think we both need it."

"I'm good with that. I'll order the food, and we can pick it up on our way home." He pushes me into my office and closes the door. "I need you to know, I love you. I've wanted to tell you that all day."

I smile, "I love you too. I know this may get a little complicated. Do you want to change positions?"

"No, I want to be near you. I'm good with where I am if that's okay with you." He leans down and kisses me. "I'll go order dinner. Get your day wrapped up, and we'll leave."

"Yes sir, you are very demanding." I pull out of his arms and head to my desk to clear up the rest of the day.

"I have a woman I have to take care of now. I'm going to be demanding. I need to make sure she takes care of herself." He moves to leave the office.

"Oh, she'll take care of herself. She has a man to take care of now."

He scoffs, "We will take care of each other, babe. Get your stuff, and let's get out of here." He leaves to order the Chinese.

Chapter 19

Alex

We are on our way to my place when my phone rings. I look at my phone...Mom...*great*. I push the button, "Hey mom."

Emily looks over at me with no expression

"Alexander, why haven't you called? What have you been up to?"

"I've been working mom. I'm fine." I roll my eyes.

Emily laughs.

"Who is that? Are you seeing someone? Who is she? What does she do?"

"Whoa...slow down mom. Good grief." I'm not sure I'm ready to tell my mom that I'm in a relationship with an older woman. How do you approach that? "I am...heading to my bosses for dinner. And..."

"With a woman? I heard her laugh. You can't keep something like this from your mother. You know I always find out what you are up to. So, what are you up to?" She never takes a breath; she just keeps squawking.

I huff out loud, "Mom, stop. I am seeing someone. She's a wonderful woman. She's the CEO of the company I work for. You'll love her."

"Woman? Just how old is this woman? CEO? Don't you work for the CEO? Are you screwing your way to the top of that company? I taught you better than that." She doesn't stop the word vomit.

"Mom, stop. She's a great person. You will love her. No, I'm not sleeping my way to the top. I'm pretty much at the top. I'll call later and we can set up a time for you to meet her. Okay?" I know this will only appease her for a short period of time. But good grief, she needs to stop asking so many questions.

"You really need to be careful with who you date, son. You know, women in the workforce are hard to handle sometimes. I saw Maddy Frazier the other day, she asked about you."

I scoff, "Mom, that's enough. Maddy was from high school. I'm twenty-five, I can get my own girl, thank you very much. Now, I've got to go. We are pulling into the Chinese place to get our food."

"Chinese? She doesn't cook? What kind of woman doesn't cook for her man? The kind that works twenty-four/seven, that's the kind. You need a sweet girl like Maddy..."

I cut her off, "I'll talk to you later mom. Bye." I hung up the phone and looked over at Emily. "Sorry about that. My mom can be a little overpowering. You'll see when you meet her."

She laughs, "It didn't sound like she wanted you to be with me. Who's Maddy?"

I snarl, "A girl I went out with in high school, like eight years ago. We parted as friends. I haven't even talked to her since graduation. My mom gets shit in her head and just goes with it. That's the way she thinks things should be."

She laughs out loud, "Your mom wants you to have a hometown girl who will cook and clean for you and take care of your every need."

"Yeah, funny. Let's get our dinner and get home. I'll show you what I really want." I wiggle my eyebrows up and down.

She is still laughing as we both get out of the car and head to the Chinese restaurant to get our orders.

Women can't live with them and can't live without them. Damn...

We had just finished dinner and settled in to watch a movie when somebody rang my doorbell.

Emily looks at me questioningly. "Are you expecting someone?"

I shrug, "No, nobody ever comes to visit me except you." I stand and make my way to the door, and when I open it, I am shocked. "Umm, mom, what are you doing here?"

"Well, are you gonna let me in or just stand there like a bump on a pickle?"

I step back, opening the door wider, and gesturing for my mom to come in.

When Emily sees her, she stands from the sofa.

I look between Emily and my mom. "Mom, this is Emily. Emily, this is my mother, Suzanne Bennett."

Emily reaches out to shake my mom's hand. "It's very nice to meet you, Mrs. Bennett."

Instead of shaking Emily's hand, Mom stares her up and down, crosses her arms over her chest, and then looks at me. "So, this is the boss you're screwing? At least she's pretty."

"Mom!" Now I'm fucking embarrassed. "Mom, that will be enough. I happen to be in love with Emily, we aren't just screwing."

Emily's arm lowers. "I'll just make myself scarce while you two have a talk." Emily steps out of the room and heads down the hallway.

I look at my mother. "That was uncalled for and rude. Why are you being so fucking rude? You're never this rude, what is wrong with you?"

She walks to the sofa and plops down. "Watch your language, young man. I do not want some hussy taking advantage of my poor baby boy."

I stand there staring at her with my hands on my hips. "Mom, you don't even know her. She isn't a hussy, I promise. She's not taking advantage of me at all. If you don't like her, that's your problem, not mine. She's a wonderful person. You should really get to know her before you start throwing accusations around."

Suzanne Bennett looks like a sophisticated pain in the ass. Her hair is always perfect, not one bleach blonde curl out of place. Her makeup is always on; she does not leave the house without it. Her clothes are impeccable, jewelry to match. She's what most people would call high society...snooty ass bitch. She runs around with the governor's wife and thinks she's somebody. When in reality, she got a large settlement when my dad passed away, like $5,000,000. So, now she makes her way around town to all of the social circles. Something she wouldn't have been caught dead doing when Dad was alive.

I look at my mom and scoff. "If you can't say anything nice, don't say anything at all. The doors over there, don't let it hit you in the ass on your way out." I point to the door.

Mom laughs, "Ohh, I'm not going anywhere. I'm gonna make sure this bitch is perfect for my son, otherwise, she's gonna be gone."

"Mom, you're not going to tell me who I can date or see if anybody's perfect for me. That is not your call; that is mine. I love Emily, and she loves me, end of story." I stomp out of the room to check on Emily. I couldn't care less whether my mother was there when I got back.

I walk into the bedroom and close the door. Emily is sitting on the edge of the bed. "I am so sorry. I am so, so very sorry. My mom is a pain in the ass. I don't know what came over her. I have no idea why she's even here. She has been to my apartment a total of three times since I moved in here three years ago. Now, all of a sudden, she shows up and wants to start telling me what I'm going to do." I start pacing back and forth, and the more I think about my mom sitting out there, the madder I get.

Emily stands, stops me from pacing, and takes me into her arms, giving me the hug I need. "She's just trying to keep your best interests at heart. Does she know that I am 15 years older than you?"

I shake my head, "No. She doesn't know how old you are I've never told her. It doesn't matter. All that matters is that we love each other. I can deal with the age difference. You can deal with the age difference. And that's all that matters."

Emily slowly nods, "But she is still your mother. What can she do to keep us apart?"

I pull back from Emily slightly. "Nothing. She can't do anything."

Emily looks into my eyes for a long moment. Then she says, "Then let's go out there and let her know we are together. We are staying together. And there's nothing she can do about it. I'm not afraid of your mother. I don't care who her best friend is. She could be friends with the queen of England for all I cared. None of that makes any difference."

I smile for the first time in thirty minutes. "This is why I love you; you don't back down."

I take her hand, and we interlock our fingers. We walk out to the living room with our heads held high. Mom is still sitting on the sofa with her arms crossed over her chest, looking somewhat disheveled.

Chapter 20

Emily

I'll be damned if I'm going to allow anyone to tell me what to do. I'm forty years old, for crying out loud.

Alex stands beside me, holding my hand. We stand in front of his mother and glare at her.

When she looks at us, her eyes travel to our hands and then back to our eyes. Her eyes shift from me to Alex and back to me. "So, you think you're good enough for my son, do you?"

I smile, "No I don't *think* I'm good enough, I know I'm good enough."

Mrs. Bennett stands, "I've had you checked out. You're not all what you say you are. From what I understand you stole a company, the poor guy was killed by the Police Department because of you, and you want to stand here and tell me that you are good enough for my son? I don't think so."

I stop Alex from going toward his mother. Looking her square in the eye, I say, "First of all, you have no idea what you're talking about. The company was given to me by the former owner. The man you say I so-called had killed by the police, was embezzling money from the company. If you wanna come after me, you better have your facts straight lady."

She looks at Alex, "Do you even know how old she is?"

He laughs, "Yes mother, I know how old she is. Age doesn't matter to me. We are compatible. We love each other. And you have no say so in this relationship. Now, I'm going to ask you one more time to please leave."

His mother stands facing us, arms crossed over her chest. Her face turns bright red. "What would your father say about this?"

Alex laughs, "He'd say good for me. I have no idea what has happened to you since dad died, but I suggest you keep your nose in your own business and out of mine. There's the door, goodbye mother."

Mrs. Bennett snatches her purse from the sofa, stomps her feet like a little girl all the way to the door, and opens it. Before she leaves, she turns and faces us. "I'll give this relationship six months. It won't last past that. And if you think about marrying my son, you'll not get one red cent of my money."

I laugh, "That's fine, I have my own money, thank you very much. I don't need yours. Alex has his own money as well. *It's been a pleasure meeting you today.*" Emily let that last part out with a little bit of sarcasm. I can't help but laugh.

His mom storms out the door, slamming it behind her.

Alex looks at me, smiles, and says, "Again I'm so sorry. I do not know what got into her, I promise, that will not happen again."

I laugh and head to the sofa. "It's fine. I kind of understand where she's coming from. I am fifteen years older than you."

He sits next to me on the sofa, takes my hand in his, and looks into my eyes. "I'm going to say this one more time, age does not matter." He places his hand over my heart. "All that matters is how we feel about each other and what is in our hearts."

I'm supposed to be the strong Emily VanZandt, but I let a tear slip out of my eye. "Thank you."

He pulls me into his body, we sit back on the sofa, and he holds me for quite a while. He finally asks, "Do you want to go ahead and watch the movie?"

Reluctantly, I say, "Sure."

He clicks the TV on, and we start watching some old horror movie.

I am not paying much attention. His mother's words keep coming back to me. *Do you even know how old she is? So, this is the boss you're screwing?* She was so mean, and she didn't even want to give me a chance. Maybe...fuck...maybe I should back away from him. Yes, it will hurt like hell, but I don't want him to have issues with his mom.

My mind is whirling. I sit there stewing over everything that transpired with his mom. I decided to go back to my place tonight. Yes, I'll go home, and then tomorrow, I will end this. It's what's best for Alex.

I know he can tell something is up. I'm stiffer next to him, not snuggling into him like I normally do. The movie finally ends. I have no idea what we watched, so I couldn't tell you if it was good or bad.

I stand and turn to face Alex. "I'm gonna go home tonight."

He stands and tries to take my hand, but I snatch it away. He puts his hands on his hips and looks at me. "I knew something was bothering you. And I'm pretty sure it was my mother. And she will not bother us again, I promise. I will not allow her to take you away from me."

I take a few more steps backward. "Alex, I'm sorry, but I do need to go home. I need to think some things through. I'm sorry. I'll see you in the morning at the office." I grab my purse off the side table by the door and sprint to the elevator. I think I push the elevator button several times, trying to get here faster, knowing that it doesn't work.

Alex is standing in the open door of his apartment, staring at me. "Emily, please don't go. Let's talk about this. I love you. You love me. That's all that matters."

I turn and stare at him for a brief moment. "That's not all that matters. We really need to think about what we're doing. I will not come between you and your family."

He is about to say something else, and the elevator doors mercifully opens. I back into the elevator not taking my eyes off his. We stare at each other until the doors close. I'm not only losing the best thing that ever happened to me in my life, but I'm losing a damn good assistant.

Tears stream down my face by the time I get to my car. My phone buzzes several times, and I know it is him. I am not going to answer it. I can't. I can't talk to him right now. I have to think this through. I have to think about what's best for both of us.

My phone keeps buzzing, and I keep ignoring it. I know it's him and I can't talk to him right now. By the time I get to my house, I'm a blubbering idiot. I pull into the drive, open the garage door, and ease my way in. I turn the car off, close the garage door, and sit in my car ugly crying. Snot and boogers everywhere. Tears streaming down my face. This has to be done. I knew it from the start. I have to tell him in the morning we can't see each other outside of work.

This has got to be the worst day of my life.

Chapter 21

Alex

This is going to be the worst night of my entire life. First, my mother and her fucking mouth, and then Emily leaving. She won't even answer my phone calls or my text messages. I've tried to call her at least fifty times, and I've sent, I know, twenty text messages with no response. This is torture, absolute torture.

How am I supposed to face her at work in the morning, knowing that she wants to call this off? All because of what my fucking mother said.

I sent one more text for the night.

Me: Emily, I'm going to make this all better. I will not be in the office in the morning. I love you.

I strip down to my boxers and crawl in my bed alone for the first time in months. My mom will pay for what she did tonight. And she will apologize to Emily.

I can't sleep; I toss and turn all night. Finally, I get up the next morning and check my phone. Still, Emily hasn't responded. I move to my bathroom, turn on the shower, and look in the mirror. My hair is standing up, my eyes are bloodshot, and I look like hell.

I quickly shower, put on my clothes, and head out the door.

After my father passed away and left my mom the life insurance policy, she sold our childhood home and bought a home in Nampa in the prestigious addition of Northwood. I do not know what is going through my mother's head. I don't know why she thinks she has to have all of this ritzy bitch ass shit, but I'm fixing to bring her down to earth.

I drive the twenty miles from Boise to Nampa, take exit 33, and make my way to Northwood edition. Why would a fifty-year-old single woman want to live alone in one of these large ass houses? Midlife crisis? I don't know, but I'm fixing to have it out with my mother.

I pull into her driveway, kill my car, get out, and walk up to the door. She gave me a key when she moved in, so I'll let myself in. She barged into my life last night and ruined my fucking night, I'm gonna barge into hers.

It's 8:00 in the morning, and I hear voices, moms and... a man? What the actual fuck is going on? I make my way to the back of the house, where the kitchen is. There's a large opening looking into the kitchen, I see mom standing at the sink chattering about something and a man sitting at the island, shirtless and in his boxers. "What the fuck is going on here?"

Mom screeches and turns as the man sitting in the chair also jumps, spilling his coffee all over the countertop—the smile on Mom's face fads. And the man in his boxers has a deer-in-the-headlights look plastered on his ugly mug, just staring at me with his mouth gaping open.

I'm standing there with my hands on my hips. "Could somebody please explain to me what the fuck is going on here?"

Mom starts toward me. "Now Alexander, don't get all upset. There's no reason for it."

Steam is rolling out of my ears at this moment because I'm furious. "The fuck you say. You had the audacity to come to my apartment last night bitching about my new girlfriend and here I find you shacking up with a man. Kinda like the pot calling the kettle black there, mom. Double standards much, mom? And who the fuck is this anyway? And how long has this been going on?"

The man in his underwear stands. "Now listen son..."

I wave my arm, "Oh, hell no, I'm not your fucking son, get your ass up and get out of my mother's house."

Mom looks at the man, "Just wait for me in the other room, Hun."

My hands are back on my hips, staring at my mother. "You have a lot of nerve, Mom. Coming into my apartment, dictating what I'm going to do and whom I'm going to see, and here you are fucking some bald asshole. Who the fuck is he?"

She clears her throat, "He's my gynecologist."

I rake my hand through my hair and start pacing back and forth. This is what my mother does to me, and she frustrates me. "Gross, Mom, that's just fucking gross. He's your gynecologist? Seriously? Who the fuck dates their gynecologist? And for how long? How long has this been going on? After what you did last night, you should be ashamed of yourself."

She holds a kitchen towel in her hand and keeps twisting it between her hands. "Alexander now don't go getting all high and mighty on me. You shouldn't be seeing a much older woman. She is so much older than you..."

"Stop...I'm not listening to this shit. You are fucking your doctor. I don't want to hear your babbling. You are a fucking hypocrite. You will be apologizing to Emily. Today!" I'm screaming. "You will get that asshole out of this house..."

"Now, that is going way too far. I am happy with George. He's a wonderful man. And he takes very good care of me." She's starting to get red in the face.

"Wow! You are such a fucking hypocrite. Fuck mom, what else have you been doing while looking down your nose at what others are doing? Tell me, how do you sleep at night?" I put my hand up, "Never mind. I don't want to know. I expect you at my office this morning. Get your ass ready. Because if you aren't there within the next two hours, I'm coming to get you and dragging your ass downtown. Do you understand me?"

"Now, Alex..."

"Stop, you are not going to be heard anymore. I'm done. Fuck whoever you want. But you will apologize to Emily. She left last night in tears. She won't speak to me."

"Good, she's not for you." Mom starts to move back toward the sink.

I raise my voice again. "Good! Really? You are shaking up with Dr. FeelGood and you have the audacity to say, good to me. How dare you? Emily is the best thing that has ever happened to me. You have two hours mom, that's it. You will apologize to her, or you will not see me again." I storm out of the kitchen and out of the house. I am so fucking pissed right now.

How dare her? Fuck! I hit the steering wheel of my car with the heel of my hand. "Fuck!" I drive straight to the city, pull into my parking spot in the garage, and head to my office. This is going to end today. I will not spend another night without my woman.

Chapter 22

Emily

I'm not sure when I finally fell asleep last night. When I woke up this morning, my eyes were red and puffy. Crying does not suit me. Why was I crying? I knew this was going to come to an end at some point. He's simply too young for me, although I want him badly, and I normally get what I want. Except in this instance, I don't think I'm going to actually get what I want this time.

I am already late for the office. When I step into the shower, all I can think about is the last time I showered. Alex was here with me. I can still feel his hands on my body as I let the hot water run over me. Why am I allowing myself to have these feelings?

By the time I get out of the shower, my fingers and toes are all wrinkly, and the tears won't stop. This is where I have to be a big girl. Pull up my big girl panties and act like the badass I am. I stare at my reflection looking back at me from the mirror. I blurt out, talking to myself. "You are a bright, intelligent woman. You can do anything. You do not need anyone, especially a man. Get your ass in gear, be the woman you are, and straighten your crown. You are the queen of your domain. You are the ruler of your universe. Now, get out of your fucking head and get back to work."

I'm not up to my normal self at all. I grab a washcloth and get it wet with freezing cold water. Wringing out the cloth, I press it firmly against my eyes, allowing the cool to rejuvenate me. I remove the cloth, get more cold water on it, wring it out again, and lie on my bed. I place the cool cloth over my entire face. I lie naked on my bed with the ceiling fan blowing down on me, cooling me down. I'm pissed at myself for being such a wimp when it comes to Alex.

That's all I need. I just need to rejuvenate. I have to remember who I am, and who I am, is a fucking badass woman who takes no prisoners in business.

I remove the washcloth from my face, sit on the edge of my bed, and contemplate whether I even want to go into the office today. *I do own the company. I am the boss. What I learned at a very young age is that when the boss is away, the employees will play.*

I let out an exasperated huff before removing my ass from the edge of the bed. I go to my closet, and I pick out one of my black dress suits and a light lavender blouse. I grab my lavender stilettos and proceed to get dressed. Whether I like it or not, I am the boss. With that comes responsibility.

I go into the bathroom and put on a light touch of makeup, trying to cover the redness and bags under my eyes. I look in the mirror, giving myself a once over. "Well, I guess that'll have to do. Let's do this."

I head to the office. The traffic's not bad at 9:00 AM. Maybe I should go in late every day. I smile to myself. That'll never happen.

I pull into the garage, not looking around, not wanting to know if *he's* here. I get to the elevator, push the button to the top floor, and let it whisk me away.

When I step off the elevator, I meet the gaze of the receptionist, Sabrina Nickle, who smiles at me. "Good morning, Ms. VanZant. You have a visitor in your office, and here are your messages."

I give her an indecisive look. "A visitor in my office. Who is it? Is Mr. Bennett not in yet?"

Her smile disappears. "Um... No ma'am, Mr. Bennett has not come in yet. The woman said she had an appointment. I apologize."

I allow myself to show her a half smile. "It's fine Sabrina, I'm sure it was on my calendar, and I just missed it, thank you. Is there anything else I need to know?"

She smiles brightly again. "No ma'am, that's all I have for you right now."

Walking to my office, I don't remember Alex booking me any appointments for this morning. Shit, did I not look at my calendar? I don't remember. Why can't I remember? I check my phone and see that I've missed a ton of text calls and have a voicemail. I can't bother with that right now if there is an appointment waiting for me.

When I get to my outside office area, there is no Alex. His desk has not been touched since yesterday. I can tell because he's a neat freak, and everything is in its place. When he's working he does leave a few things out. So, where could he be?

I shake my head and make it through the door to my office. I notice a woman standing by the window, looking out. She looks a little familiar, but I can't place her. Then she turns around. Well, that's just fucking great, Mrs. Bennett.

Letting out a slight sigh, I address her. "Mrs. Bennett, what do I owe the pleasure of this visit?"

She walks directly to me, gets in my personal space, and says, "You're looking well this morning Emily. I need to talk to you about what happened last night. You have to understand Alex is my only son. I have to look out for him. I have to make sure that what he's doing and who he's doing is right for him. I need to make sure it's not somebody who's going to just try and take him for everything he has."

I sigh, "I mean no disrespect Mrs..."

She cut me off. "Oh, I'm sure you don't mean any disrespect, but by dating my son, who is so much younger than you, you are disrespecting me. You are disrespecting my wishes. You are disrespecting everything about my family..."

This time, I stop her. "That is quite enough, just shut up," I say, letting out a long breath.

She folds her arms over her chest and gives me a stern look. "Again, you disrespect me by telling me to shut up."

I fold my arms over my chest, squarely looking her in the eye, and say, "I will not tolerate you coming in here and yelling at me. I am with Alex because we want to be with each other. If he didn't he would tell me. You have no right to tell him what to do. He is a grown ass man. He can do whatever he wants. You wanna take me on lady, bring it."

Stepping back slightly and giving me a snarling look. "You have no idea who you're dealing with, lady."

I smile, "And you have no idea who you're dealing with."

She huffs, "My lawyers will be in touch with you shortly." She turns and heads for the door.

I yell back at her over my shoulder, "They'll need to contact my attorney. Welby, Stout, and Bingham, your lawyer will need to talk to Bill Welby."

She stops dead in her tracks, turns, and faces me once again. "Well, isn't this interesting? Bill happens to be a very dear friend of mine. I'm sure my business will be way more important to him than yours."

I laugh, "I guess we'll find out now won't we. Have a good day Mrs. Bennett."

She chuckles as she leaves the office.

My heart is racing, and I want to punch something. Just then, my phone rings. I pick it up and look to see who is calling. I press the answer button. "Hello Alex. You'll never guess who just left the office."

All he says is, "Fuck!"

Chapter 23

Alex

I ran a hand down my face as Emily described what had just happened between her and my mother.

"I'll take care of her. And how is she really good friends with Bill Welby. I've never even heard his name until I came to work for you. I bet she's bluffing. I have an idea. Order from the Italian restaurant and have it delivered at 6:00 PM tonight. My mother and her new boyfriend are going to be invited to dinner."

I hear Emily let out a slow breath. "Are you sure that's such a good idea? I mean, should we even try this, Alex? Maybe she's right."

"The hell she is. I love you. Do you love me?" I wait a long moment for her answer.

She finally answers. "Yes, Alex, I love you. Are we really going to do this?"

"Yes. Now, order the food for tonight. We are settling this tonight. It's the only way I can get my mother to shut up. I'll see you tonight at 6:00. I've got some things I need to do today."

There is silence on the phone for a brief moment. "Okay, we'll try it your way this time and see what happens, but I'm calling Bill to give him a heads-up."

I let out a slow breath. "Okay, that might be a good idea. I will see you tonight."

The call ends.

I look at my phone, and I push my mother's number.

She answers with a bright, cheerful greeting. "Oh, good morning, son. I'm so glad you called me. I need to talk to you."

"Well, you're awfully chipper this morning mom. I guess you got laid last night."

"Now that will be quite enough from you, young man." She let out a huff of exasperation.

I shake my head, not that she could see it. "I didn't call to fight or argue. I called to invite you and your new boyfriend over to my place tonight for dinner, 6:00 PM, be there."

She stutters out, "Ohhhh, I'm really not...um... I'm not sure that's going to work."

I laugh out loud, "It is not up for discussion. I'll see you and your doctor friend at 6:00 PM. Bye mother." I hang up the phone before she can say anything else.

My mother is a pain in the fucking ass. She had better show up with the new boyfriend. I'm so sick of this shit.

I shoot a text to Emily: **Mom and boyfriend will be there at 6:00.**
Emily: ohh fun...lol
Me: lol... Don't you know it. I'll see you then.

The rest of my day consisted of getting a haircut, running by the grocery store, and the liquor store.

5:30 p.m. that night

I arrive at my place, and Emily is there waiting for me. I give her a kiss as I step into the kitchen. "You look beautiful. You didn't have to get dressed up for my mother. She's a bitch, and we are going to straighten this whole thing out tonight."

My girl is wearing a cute sundress with wide straps across her beautiful shoulders and a pair of cute low-flat sandals. "I wanted everything to be perfect. She doesn't like me as it is, so this is at least me being low-key." She smiles her glorious smile at me.

I put the bags I carried in on the counter.

"What's all this? I ordered from the restaurant you told me to order from." Her face is scrunched up, and she looks so fucking cute.

"I know. I got some desert and wine. I thought it would go well with the food tonight. Oh, and I got a haircut. What do ya think?" I turn my head from side to side, letting her see it from all directions.

She laughs, "It looks very distinguished. Are you trying to prove something with all this?"

"Nah, just wanted to look good for my woman tonight." I pull her into me and give her a very long, lingering kiss. I move my tongue across the slit of her lips, and she opens for me.

Our tongues mingle as if we had been doing this for years. She is my other half, my soulmate.

Just as my dick is getting hard, the doorbell rings. I pull back slightly, "Shit, I am not ready for this."

She glances down at my pants and my growing dick. "I see that. You better take care of that before your mother sees it." She begins to laugh hard.

The mention of my mother did the trick. It deflated almost instantly. "Fuck, let's get this over with." I take her hand, kiss the back of it, and say, "After this, we never spend another night apart."

She takes a deep breath, nods, and says, "I agree. Let's do this. Stick by me and we will make it through."

I give her another quick peck on the lips, and we head to the door together, hand in hand.

When we open the door, my mother is decked out in the most god-awful orange moo-moo thing, with her hair piled high on her head and a pair of old flat sandals. The man standing next to her almost looks sorry to be here.

I stick my hand out to him, "Welcome. Please come in."

He shakes my hand, and they walk in.

We all stand in the foyer staring at each other for a very long moment before the man finally says, "I'm George. We didn't formally meet yesterday."

"Yes, it's nice to meet you. This is my girlfriend, Emily VanZant," I introduce them.

Emily extends her hand out, "It's nice to meet you, George."

"VanZant? Are you related to Marianne VanZant?" George asks.

She clears her throat, "Yes, that was my mother."

He nods, "She was a wonderful friend of mine. I'm so sorry for your loss."

My mom is giving poor George go-to-hell looks. She then looks at Emily, "How long have your parents been dead?"

God, she's the rudest person on earth. "Mom!"

Emily put her hand on my arm, "It's fine. My mom has been gone for about five years. She was killed in a car accident on I-80. My father left when I was small, and I didn't know him."

Mom clears her throat, "Sorry about that. So, are we just going to stand here all night and stare at each other or eat?"

"Mom, stop it. You are being so rude." I step to the side, "Come on in. Make yourselves comfortable in the living room. George, would you like a drink? I'm having a Scotch on the Rocks."

George smiles, "Yes, that would be nice. Thank you."

"Mom, wine?"

"Whatever you have is fine." She dismisses me, "I don't want to put you out."

I roll my eyes and head to the wet bar in the corner of the living room.

George looks so lost—poor guy.

Mixing our drinks, I look at George, "What is it you do again?"

Emily walks back into the room just as George answers.

"Gynecologist," he says matter-of-factly.

Emily stops dead in her tracks. "Dr. Stucky?"

"I wasn't sure you recognized me. Yes, Emily, it's me," he confirms.

Great, my mother's new boyfriend is my girlfriend's doctor. "How do you two know each other?"

Emily looks from him to me, "He found my mother's ovarian cancer in time to save her life. I'm sorry, Dr. Stucky, I didn't recognize you without the scrubs and hat that you wear during surgery."

He waves his hand, "Don't worry about it. It was a stressful time. I'm glad she had the extra time."

Emily looks a bit out of sorts, "Excuse me for a moment."

Mother gasps, "Are we eating dinner or talking about dead people for the rest of the night?"

George looks at my mother, "Evelyn, stop being so rude. That young lady is a very nice person. You made her out to be some gold digger. She's not, she has her own money."

Mom scoffs, "Just whose side are you on, anyway?"

"I'm on the side of right. And you, my dear, are not right. I love you, but you will not treat people this way." George looks at me as I hand him his drink. "I'm sorry for your mother's bad behavior. She has it in her mind that Emily is after her money."

I look confused. "What money? She spent most of Dad's life insurance on that house, I thought."

She laughs, "You know you have a large trust settlement left to you from your grandfather. I have made some very wise investments that have landed me a short windfall. I'm sure your *woman* knows exactly what you're worth. She's probably had you investigated."

There is a clearing of a throat behind the sofa, and we all turn to see Emily. Her face is so red, I thought it might explode.

She licks her lips, then proceeds to tell the room, mostly my mother, just what she thought. "I am not after anyone's money. I have not had Alex investigated for any reason. I have no idea what you are talking about, and for the record, my net worth is 1.6 billion dollars."

I laugh when I see my mother's face.

Mom snorts, "Just where did you get your fortune from, missy?"

"Not that it's any of your business, but my mom had sizable life insurance policies. You aren't the only one who can make sound investments. I also make over five hundred thousand dollars a year. My company is now on the top ten list for best software in the world. Now, I think I will excuse myself for the evening. I'm all of a sudden not hungry." Emily storms off to the bedroom.

I glare at my mother. "You are a nasty person. When did you become this self-righteous, self-centered person? You used to be a very loving woman. Where did my mother go?"

George looks at Mom, "If you are going to continue to be a nasty woman, I don't want to be around you. I fell in love with the bright, sophisticated, loving woman I've known for years. Not this nasty ass bitch that you have been tonight. You've not treated anyone with such disrespect since we've been together."

Mom's face softens at George's words. "Oh George, I really thought she was after his, my money."

I look at her, "How would she have known you had all that money? She isn't a snoop. And while we are on the subject, I thought you said you had her looked into. If you had her investigated, you would have known how much she was worth. I didn't even know how much she was worth until tonight."

I turn to George. " If you are hungry, the kitchen is that way." I point to the back of the apartment. "I'm going to check on Emily."

Mom's voice pipes up before I get to the bedroom. "Please ask her to come back."

I turn and look at her, "Not if you are going to continue to treat her like shit."

She shakes her head, "I'm not. Please, ask her to come back in here."

"I'll ask her, but don't hold your breath after that stellar performance." I get to the bedroom door and open it to find Emily sitting on the edge of the bed.

"Are they gone?" She looks at me.

"No, Mother would like to talk to you. She wants you to come back out." I sit down next to her. "You don't have to. Not after what she did and said. But for the record, her voice sounded more like its old self. She may want to apologize."

She wipes her eyes, "I love Dr. Stucky. But your mother..."

"Trust me, I know. Look, give her one more chance, and if it doesn't work out, we do not have to see her again. I think poor George is on the verge of breaking up with her. He's furious." I take her hand in mine. "One more chance for me?"

She laughs softly, "Fine. Let me clean up my face, and I'll be out."

I kiss her cheek, "Thank you. I love you."

She looks at me and smiles. "I'm doing this because I love you. Give me a few minutes. Please pour me a huge glass of wine, pretty please."

I laugh, "I'll find the biggest glass we have." I walk back out to the living room.

God, what a fucking night.

Chapter 24

Emily

After Alex leaves the room and begs me to come back out, I go to the bathroom to check my makeup. Thank God for waterproof mascara. I reapply some of my makeup and straighten my hair. I look at my reflection in the mirror and give myself a really good pep talk.

"Okay, girl, you've got this. Nobody has ever talked to you the way Mrs. Bennett talked to you. You will not allow that again. You will be the strong ass woman that you are, and you will stand up for yourself. You do not *need* a man, but you really do want the man that's out there. So, let's do this."

I run my hands over my dress, straightening out the wrinkles that aren't there. I throw my shoulders back, and I walk out of the bedroom with more confidence than I am feeling.

As I walk down the hallway, I can hear their voices. Everyone seems to be talking in normal voices now, which is a good thing. When I get to the end of the hall, Dr. Stucky and Alex are laughing at something, and what's that? Mrs. Bennett has a smile on her face. Hmm.

I clear my throat as I walk in.

Alex gets up from his seat, walks over to me, and takes me in his arms, kissing me on the cheek. "Thank you so much," he whispers.

I smile, "Let's just see how this goes," whispering back to him.

Alex and I walk back over to the seating area, and Dr. Stucky stands and shakes my hand. Dr. Stucky smiles, "Emily, thank you for returning." he looks back at Mrs. Bennett, then at me again. "And we are all going to be on our best behavior."

Then, Mrs. Bennett stands, walks toward me, and says, "I would like to apologize for my actions. I know I've been unreasonable and ill-mannered, and I very much would like to apologize."

I give her a stoic smile, "Thank you Mrs. Bennett. I do appreciate that. I hope moving forward, we can try to be friends."

"Emily, I do still have some concerns. However, my son has assured me that they are unfounded concerns. I had no idea about the company and how you acquired it. I was told a lot of different information. So, from now on, I will not assume anything."

"Thank you. Now, who's hungry?" Emily smiles and looks around at everyone.

Everyone laughs.

Dr. Stucky chuckles, "I'm starving. When I heard Alex was getting food from the Italian restaurant, I was absolutely excited. I love that place." He rubs his hands together like an excited little boy.

Mrs. Bennett laughs, "Calm down, Hun. We won't let you starve." She looks at me, "Do you need any help in the kitchen?"

I shake my head, "No I've got everything prepared, it's just in the warmer. Alex, can you pour the wine for everyone. Let's all have a seat at the dining room table."

I put all the food on the table as everyone takes their seats. Alex sets the very full wine glasses at each place setting. We sit, eat, and chit-chat during the entire dinner. It is definitely an about-face from earlier in the evening.

All in all, the evening ended quite well. Mrs. Bennett stopped making snide remarks and side glances at me about halfway through dinner. Alex and Dr. Stucky seem to hit it off quite nicely. Apparently, he and Mrs. Bennett have been seeing each other for quite a while and she just never told Alex.

When everyone leaves, the dishes are cleaned and put away, and we head to bed.

Alex pulls me into him, "I think that ended well. Let's celebrate."

"We just had several bottles of wine. Just how do you want to celebrate? I'm not sure your mother is fully convinced that we love each other. She was still side eyeing me during dinner."

He laughs, moves his hand to my butt, and says, "I do not want to talk about my mother. I want to eat you and fuck you senseless."

I make my mouth form the 'O', and my lip twitches up. "I see. You want the sexual favor celebration." I push back from him, reach around, and unfasten my skirt, letting it slide to the floor. I kick it off to the side with my heeled shoe. I start to remove my shoes.

"No, leave them on." He gives me a devilish smile.

"Oh, Mr. Bennett, you are learning so quickly. I gather you like a *slutty boss*." I give air quotes around the slutty boss.

He laughs, "Ms. VanZant, I like you any way you want to be. But yes, slutty boss tonight would be awesome. Tell me, Ms. VanZant, what can I do for you?"

"Oh my." I remove my blouse, pushing my breasts up and out. I move my hand to my right breast and start to finger my nipple through the thin lace. "I think you should start at the top and work your way down."

He licks his lips and starts to move toward me.

I put up a finger. "Wait, not yet. I want you to be completely naked. Remove your shirt first."

His eyes are extraordinarily dark. Slowly, he begins to unbutton his shirt. When he removes it, he tosses it to the side.

"Now your pants."

He smiles, unbuckles his pants, and pushes them over his hips. He kicks his shoes off as well.

I lick my lips, "Oh my, that is quite a large tent you have there in those boxers. You might want to remove those and free that enormous package."

He does as he is told, freeing his glorious cock.

"Mr. Bennett, you are very well put together. You are," moving toward him, taking his dick in my hand, "very well..." I clear my throat, "...endowed."

His hand moves over mine, holding it around his very hard cock, and starts moving my hand up and down his massive shaft. "Can I taste you yet?"

I move my other hand from my breast to my crotch, "You want this? You want to taste me...here?"

I finger myself, getting my fingers nice and juicy.

"Very much so," he starts toward me again.

I lift my gaze to him, "You can taste me here." I rub my juices on my lips.

He gets close enough to kiss me. His lips, on mine, fast, hard, and needy. He moans when he tastes me.

I continue stroking his hardness. Moving my hand over the tip, I smear the pre-cum up and down his shaft. I think he got harder if that's possible.

His lips leave mine and move to the crook of my neck, where he nibbles, kisses, and gives a slight bite. As he continues to move down, he takes one of my breasts in his hand and bites my nipple, then licks and sucks it into his mouth.

I let out a loud moan and allowed him to continue his kissing-biting assault on my body.

Alex moves me backward toward the bed as he kisses my neck, sucks on my earlobe, and moves his mouth around on my shoulder.

My knees hit the bed, I fall on my butt, and Alex looks down at me.

"Push back on the bed and tell me what you want. Give me explicit instructions. I need to learn what you want and like." He gives me a beautiful, devilish smile.

I push myself back up on the bed, position myself on the pillows, and spread my legs. I look at Alex, move my hand to my clit, "Suck here first."

Alex puts his knees on the bed, keeps his eyes on mine, and positions himself between my thighs. "Spread wide, baby, I'm going to devour you." His lips find my hard nub, suck it into his mouth, and begin to lick and suck harder.

"Fuck, yeah. Finger...my...pussy." I instruct between pants.

He licks around my clit, sucks it into his mouth, and plunges a finger inside my already wet channel. "Like that?"

Letting out a moan, I say, "Oh yeah. Move it in and out. Then add a finger...fuck yeah."

His hand moves as his fingers manipulate my wet smooth pussy. His tongue assaults my clit.

"Two...fingers in ... my pussy... pinky in my ass...slowly. Don't stop...sucking...fuck yeah...fuck...fuck...fuck!"

I feel him get his pinky wet with my juices, and he moves it to the opening of my back hole. He gently begins to insert his pinky in my ass, his two fingers are moving in and out of my pussy, and that fucking tongue...shit...he sucked me into his mouth.

"Fuck, yes...God...yes...I'm coming."

With all that's going on, my body shivers as my release explodes.

"Good girl, that was amazing, baby." His hand and fingers continue to move in and out of my pussy and ass while he plants kisses and bites around my clit before sucking into his mouth again.

"Fuck...you are so good...I'm coming again...damn..." my body shakes from the massive orgasm.

"I need to be inside you...now," Alex removes his fingers, mouth, and tongue from my very sensitive core.

I feel the loss when he's on top of me, plunging his hard as fuck dick into my pussy. "Yes, God, you feel so good. Your dick feels so good."

Alex looks at me as he slowly pushes into my wetness. "You are so fucking amazing. Your pussy wraps around my dick so perfectly. Come for me again." He begins to push in and out of me faster and harder.

I grab his back, scratching up as he pounds into me.

"Fucking, come baby."

Wrapping my legs around his waist, I pull him inside me deeper. "Now, I'm fucking…coming now." I coat his dick with my essence.

He slows, "That's a good girl." He kisses my nose, and then his mouth finds mine. His tongue slowly moves around in my mouth as he continues to push inside me slower now.

My arms snake around his neck, pulling him as close to me as possible. I lift my hips to meet each of his thrusts.

He pulls back, "I need to come inside you."

I nod, "Yes, come baby."

His thrusts begin to move faster and faster, "Come with me…fucking come with me now."

We both let our release go.

He pulls me into him, holding me, letting every bit of his cum fill me.

I hold onto him, reveling in the love that we share.

After a few minutes, he pulls up, looks into my eyes, and says, "I love you."

A tear slips from the corner of my eye, "I love you too."

He gives me a beautiful, long kiss before pulling out of me. He rolls to his side, pulling me with him.

I roll into his side and pull the blanket up over our cooling bodies.

My life is now complete.

Chapter 25
Alex

Six Weeks Later

My life has changed so much over the past several months. I've been working for this woman for over a year, and never in my wildest dreams would I have imagined that we would have a fantastic life together.

We made it through Chet, my mother, and the office gossip. Yeah, there was some, but not much.

Today, I'm being transferred. The board recommended that I not be directly under Emily, so they suggested moving me to another department. After Emily argued with them for hours during a very long meeting, she finally gave in. I'll be moving to the CFO's office. I'll just be down the hallway.

Mr. Streeter has proven himself to be a team player and Emily felt it would be a good move. Mr. Streeter is looking forward to having someone who isn't interested in causing him issues with his wife. His last assistant nearly caused a divorce between the two. After Emily and I had the Streeters over for dinner, she was able to explain we were still weeding out the old stuff that Chet hired. Mrs. Streeter was definitely calmer and forgiving to her husband.

We now have a pretty well-oiled machine here at Nordic. It's moving up in the software industry and constantly innovating to create better products.

I'm packing up my desk and Emily hasn't made it to her office yet. I'm getting a little worried. She was supposed to be here about an hour ago.

Mr. Streeter rounds the corner and heads my way. "Hey, Mr. Bennett, are you ready to get moved?"

I chuckle a little, "I guess so. Are you ready to have a trustworthy assistant?"

"Damn straight. Do you need any help?" Brandon asks.

"Nah, I've about got it all finished. Have you seen Emily?" I look at him.

"Not in the last couple of hours. She left our meeting and said she was heading to see Mr. Triplett. I'm not sure what that was all about though." He shoves his hands in his pockets and bobs back and forth on his feet.

I look at him. "Are you okay? You seem nervous. Are you okay with me being your assistant?"

He pulls one hand out of his pocket and waves it through the air. "Oh, shoot yeah. Like I said, Sarah is thrilled that you are going to be out there instead of hot pants happy butt that was there before."

I laugh, "Hot pants happy butt? What the hell, man?"

He chuckles, "Sarah gave her that name along with a few others I can't repeat at the office."

I just shake my head.

Brandon Streeter is tall—not slender, but not big. He has thinning brown hair with a hint of grey at the temples. He's taller than I am by about three inches. He always dresses in a nice suit. Today, he has on his brown suit, brown and tan striped tie, and tan shirt. His shoes match his tan belt. He's a funny guy, and I think we'll get along just fine.

I put the last box of stuff on the cart that I've been loading next to my desk. Putting my hands on my hips, I say, "Well that's it. I guess I'm all yours now. I wanted to talk to Emily before I left. I guess I'll catch her later." I start to push the cart.

"I'll walk with you. She's around somewhere. She'll probably wait until you are completely finished organizing your desk then she'll show up," he laughs.

I laugh too, "Probably."

We make our way down the long hallway and turn the corner that leads to the CFOs office. When we get to the office, I park the cart next to my new desk.

Brandon looks at me and says, "Hey, can you come into my office for a minute? I need your opinion about something."

I shrug, "Sure." I follow him to his door.

He opens it and steps aside.

I hear a lot of screaming and congratulations and people are everywhere. "What's this?"

Emily emerges from the crowd. "It's your party for getting to move over here. You didn't think I would let you get away from me without throwing you a party, did you?"

"Emily, I'm just around the corner."

She laughs. "I don't care. You deserve the best. Brandon allowed me to use his office to throw this little get-together. Sarah helped." She pointed to the woman standing in the corner, smiling.

I wave at Sarah and mouth thank you.

She waves back as Brandon makes his way toward her.

There are streamers, balloons, and a cake. Many people I've worked with over the year are standing around laughing and looking at Emily and me.

I smile and pull Emily into me. "I know we are at work, but this is so awesome of you to do. Thank you."

She gives me a peck on the cheek. "You are welcome. Now let's have cake."

I laugh, "Okay, sounds good."

We celebrate for about an hour before people started leaving. It was the end of Friday, and everyone was ready to get out of here. My new official day will be Monday, but moving today will make it easier to come in on Monday to a new everything.

Brandon and Sarah approached us while we were finishing up the cleaning of his office. Brandon smiled, "Don't expect this kind of treatment in the future."

We all laugh.

I smiled back at him, "Oh man, I was certain this was *an every-month* thing. Party in the boss's office. You know, kick up your heels a bit, boss."

Brandon laughs, "Starting Monday, you will be doing a lot, but kicking up your heels is not one of them."

Sarah giggles, "Do you guys want to get together this weekend? Maybe come over for dinner Saturday night?"

Emily looks at me and then answers, "That sounds fun. We'd love to. Just shoot me a text with your time and if you want me to bring anything. Thank you both so much for your understanding of our relationship and your friendship."

Sarah pulls Emily in for a hug. "You bet."

Brandon looks at Sarah, "You ready to head home?"

"Sure thing," she turns to Emily and I, "See you tomorrow night."

We both smile and say we can't wait.

Emily hugs Sarah one more time.

Brandon and I shake hands.

We all part ways. The office is clean, and we are heading out the door. I pull my girl to my side when we get on the elevator. "Thank you."

Her smile radiates the space. "You are welcome. When we get home, you are all mine."

"With pleasure."

We walk into the living room of Emily's house. I moved in about a month ago so we could quit going back and forth. It was becoming a bit much.

Emily turns to me as she starts to walk toward the kitchen. "Um, would you like to play, or are you too tired?

"I'm never too tired to play with you." I reach her in about three steps. "Lead the way, madam.

As she walks down the hall to the door that leads to her favorite room in the house, I watch her ass. I think she's shaking it more than normal for my benefit.

She opens the door, walks in, and turns to me. Her face has changed. She is now the seductress. Her eyes are dark, her mouth forms a small smile, and her gaze is on my crotch.

"See something you want?" I ask her as I begin to walk closer.

She bites her lower lip before speaking. "You were such a good boy today. I want to reward you. Tell me, what would please you most?"

The corner of my mouth quirks up. "To see you naked bent over that table."

"But what if I don't want to do that? Will you punish me?" She begins to back up toward the table.

"Maybe. But if you comply, I will keep the punishment to a minimum. You deserve a spanking for that surprise party thing anyway." I walk to the wall that has some items hanging from it and grab the leather-strapped crop. When I turn back around, she's naked.

"Just like I want you, bare ass naked. Baby, you are one in a million. Now, bend over like a good girl, take your punishments." I motion with my head toward the table.

"Punishments...plural?" She has a questioning look.

I smile, "Yes, but I think you'll like everything. What's your safe word?"

"Red." She turns and bends over, chest on the table, hands spread out to her side, and that beautiful ass sticking up in the air.

I walk up behind her, squeeze one ass cheek, then slap it and then rub my hand over the reddened area, soothing it.

She wasn't expecting that. She gasps.

"Spread those beautiful thighs as wide as you can."

She doesn't comply.

I slap the other ass cheek, smoothing it afterward.

"Spread your fucking legs."

This time, she does as she's told.

"Gorgeous. I love your ass." I slap her butt with the crop.

She moans.

I do it again.

More moaning, and her head pops up.

"You like that, don't you."

"Umhm."

I run my hand down her back, pressing my thumb into her ass slit and tracing my movements with the crop before hitting her ass with it.

"Are you wet?"

"Yes."

"You'd better check. I want you fucking dripping."

She moves her hand between her legs, moves her finger so that she penetrates her slit, and begins to move her hand so that her finger is sliding in and out of her pussy.

"Good girl." I slap her with the crop on the ass. "Let me taste."

She pulls her finger from her wetness and holds it up.

I move so that I'm beside her. Then I lick her finger and suck all the juices off. "God, you taste so amazing. I think I need more."

Removing my shirt, I rub her ass. I remove my pants, then rub her ass on the other side. I remove my boxers and step behind her. I plunge my finger inside her wetness.

She gasps and then moans with excitement.

"Oh yeah, you like that don't you?"

"Yes...fuck yes." She's almost panting.

"Come for me, baby. Come all over my hand." I plunge deeper and harder, adding another finger, "Come for me."

Her hands grab the sides of the table, she throws her head back and growls out her release. "Ffffuuuuccccckkkk!!!!"

"Such a good girl. Fuck," I pull my hand to my mouth and suck all her juices from each finger. "You taste so good. Do you want to taste me?"

She nods, "Yes, please."

"Stand up, turn and face me. Now, tell me what you want."

"I want to suck your cock until you cum in my mouth." She starts to move toward me. "Sit on the table."

We have now reversed roles. I do as she says.

"Safe word." She demands.

"Pineapple." I smile.

She snorts. "Spread your legs, stroke your cock, I'll be right back." She moves like a cat, slinking toward the toy chest.

I love the toy chest.

When she returns, she has a cock ring, "You will wear this until I say you are ready to come. Put it on."

I take the ring, slide it down my shaft, and it's tight. I look at her.

"Lie down, hold your dick straight up with one hand."

I do as she says.

She pulls her hair back, puts it in a small ponytail, and licks her lips.

Chapter 26

Emily

"You are such a good boy. That massive dick is mine. All mine." I click a button.

He looks at me, "What the fuck?"

"Vibrates..." I smile.

"I won't last long, you better get busy." He lies back on the table.

"I'm in charge and you will come when I say you come. Now, play nice or I won't let you come at all." My voice is very demanding.

He lets out a snort.

Placing one hand on the table next to Alex, I grab his balls with my other hand and squeeze slightly.

Another moaning snort.

Precum is seeping from the tip of his cock. I lower my mouth and swipe my tongue over the tip tasting his cum. "You taste so good."

Removing my hand from the table, I slide it up his torso, pinching and twisting his nipple.

"Oh fuck!"

Slowly, I lower my mouth down over his shaft, taking all of him all the way to the base. I massage his balls as my mouth torments his dick. Moving up and down, slow then fast, sucking at the tip, I can feel the vibration from the cock ring. He won't last long. I click the button on my remote. It speeds up.

"Oh fuck...you better hurry." He's about to lose it.

I smile, "Not yet." My mouth slides down over his hardness again, slowly moving down. I suck and swallow at the same time.

His hands go to my hair. His hips begin to pound up into my mouth. He's going to come whether I'm ready for him to or not.

I click the button again and turn off the cock ring.

"What...are you trying to torture me?"

"Mmmhmm."

"Fuck!"

My grip on his balls tightens and retracts over and over. His dick in my mouth, I'm moving faster and faster. He's now thrusting hard into my mouth. "I'm coming...fuck...!!!"

His sweet and salty taste flows down my throat, coating it with his essence.

"Mmmmm." I couldn't say anything else with a mouth full of dick.

I swallow, lick my lips, and come up to meet his gaze.

"When the fuck did you get a vibrating cock ring?"

I smile, "It came in yesterday. I've been dying to try it out. Did you like it?"

"It was different. It certainly progressed things a lot faster than I had anticipated."

I laugh out loud so hard it almost echoes through the room.

He starts laughing, too. His dick is still hard. "You want this." He strokes himself a few times.

"Always."

He pulls me up on the table, I straddle his lap, and his dick is in my pussy in seconds.

"Oh man, that feels good." I throw my head back and marvel at the satisfaction that I can make this man hard, and he stays hard. Fuck yeah.

I begin to move up and down on his shaft, sitting down hard and making him moan in satisfaction. I wrap my arms around his neck.

He has his arms wrapped around my waist.

I'm moving up and down on his shaft faster and harder each time I move up and down. "Fuck...I'm coming...fuck!" my release spews all down his cock.

"Oh fuck, yeah. Now it's my turn. Hold on," he moves so fast I have no idea how.

I'm now on my back, lying on the table, his dick never left me, and he's on top, thrusting hard and deep inside me. "Yes...fuck yes...come!"

After several thrusts and moans, he pushes inside me hard one last time and growls.

My walls tighten around his hardness as he lets out his final release. "Fuck! You are amazing." He kisses my nose as he falls on top of me.

I giggle, "So are you."

We don't move for several minutes. Just looking into each other's eyes. Then he finally says, "I love you more than anything in this life. You complete me from the inside out."

I smile, "I love you too. You complete me, heart, body, and soul."

His mouth is down on mine, sliding his tongue inside my mouth, and we kiss for several very long minutes.

When he pulls back from this kiss, he says, "let's go get cleaned up. I'm suddenly hungry and tired."

I laugh, "me too."

We move around the room, gather up our clothes, and head to the bedroom to get cleaned up.

I watch Alex move around the kitchen, fixing food for us. He's a strong man in his prime, and I'm so glad he picked me.

After dinner, we snuggle on the sofa to watch TV. At some point, I fall asleep peacefully.

Alex has been with Brandon for the past two weeks and I know he's not far, but I miss him just outside my door. My new assistant, Jessica, is fantastic. She picked up on everything while training with Alex. She is so organized and hasn't missed a beat since she started. I'm thankful to have her. I just miss him.

We've been hanging out with Brandon and Sarah more and more. I love them both. They have become such good friends to us. They understand our situation, only in reverse. Brandon is several years older than Sarah, fourteen to be exact. So they understand better than most.

As I was walking down the hall toward my office, I started feeling very hot. My stomach lurched, and all I could think of was to run to the bathroom. I barely made it before puking in the toilet.

Jessica comes running in, "Ms. VanZant, are you okay? Can I get you anything?"

"A wet paper towel and some water, please." I barely got that out before another wave of nausea took over.

She passes me a cold, wet towel under the stall door. "I'll run and get you some cold water. Hang on. Do I need to get Alex?"

I press the cold towel to the back of my neck. "No, I'll be fine. It must have been what I had for lunch. It was chicken salad. I will not have that again."

I heard her giggle. "I'll be right back with that water."

"Thank you."

As I'm sitting on the floor of the bathroom, my mind goes to the chicken salad I had for lunch. The mayo must have been bad. I flush the toilet and push myself up from the floor. I step out of the stall and walk to the mirror. Looking at my reflection in the mirror, I look very pale. Shit.

Jessica comes back in with the water and hands it to me. "I brought you some crackers as well. Sometimes when I get sick to my stomach they help." She hands those to me as well.

I give her a grateful look, "Thank you so much." I open the water and sip on it for a few minutes. Then I open the crackers and nibble on one.

"If you don't need anything else, I'm going to head back to my desk. I have a few things to finish up before the end of the day."

"I'm fine, Jessica. Thank you so much. And please, don't say anything to anyone. If someone is looking for me, just let them know I'm away from my desk at the moment."

She nods, "I'll do that." Then, she leaves the restroom.

I take the towel, rewet it with cold water, and press it to the back of my neck again. It seems to help. I take a few more sips of water and throw the rest of the crackers in the trash as I leave the room. I head back to my desk.

I look at my phone and pull up the app that has my monthly cycle. No, I haven't missed anything. I'm a couple of days late, but that's normal for me, so that's a good thing. I shake it off and finish my work for the day.

Brandon and Alex are going to look at some golf carts that Brandon wants to buy after work, so I'm on my own to get home.

As soon as I walk in the door, the nausea hits me again. What the hell? I run to the bathroom in my bedroom. I don't throw up, but I sure feel like I do. Is there a stomach bug going around? I hardly ever get sick. I'll call the doctor in the morning. I do not have time to be sick.

Shit!

Chapter 27

Alex

Brandon and I take separate vehicles to the golf cart place so we can just go home afterward. He finds a sweet four-seater. We are playing golf on Saturday and riding in a sweet, nice new golf cart.

I pull into the driveway, and the lights are off. It's only seven; surely she isn't asleep already. I make my way into the house, and Emily is nowhere to be found.

Walking to the kitchen, there is a note on the bar.

Alex,

I'm sorry I didn't have anything fixed for your dinner. I wasn't feeling well and I'm in bed. Please don't wake me. I feel like shit.

Love Emily

I rush down the hallway to check on her. I creep very slowly into the room, the only light shining is from the bathroom, and the door is almost closed. I walk to the bed. She's sleeping soundly. I put my hand on her forehead, and she doesn't feel feverish, that's good. I'll insist that she see a doctor tomorrow.

Making my way to the bathroom, I get dressed for bed. It's still early, so I quietly go to the kitchen to find some food. It may be a long night.

I must have fallen asleep on the sofa. Emily gently shakes my arm, and I am awakened. My eyes flutter open. "Em, how are you feeling?"

"I'm still not feeling great. I've put a call in to Dr. Stucky. He'll call me back. I just hope he doesn't say anything to your mom about me being sick." She sits down next to me on the edge of the sofa.

"He won't or I'll kick his ass. That's against some law isn't it?" I sit up slightly, resting on my elbow.

"Yeah, but now that we are all practically family, does it still apply?" She gives me a slight smile.

"Hell yeah, it still applies. So help me...maybe you should find a new doctor." I put my hand on her arm.

"No, I trust him. He was so good when my mom had cancer. I feel like I owe him somehow. Anyway, I'm not going in this morning. Tell Jessica I'll work from home and if she needs me, call me. I'm going to lie back down." She bends over, kissing me gently on the cheek. "I love you."

"I love you too. Do you want me to stay home?"

"No! Go to work. You would drive me nuts if you were here all day. I love you, but when I'm sick, I need quiet, alone, and no distractions."

I try not to look disappointed. "Fine, but you call me if anything happens and call me when you find out what George says and..."

"I will call you, I promise. Now get ready for work." She walks back to the bedroom.

Emily

I crawl back into bed just as my cell goes off.

"Hello."

"Emily, it's George. What's the matter?"

"I don't know. Food poisoning maybe. I had chicken salad yesterday and I got sick after I ate it."

"Why don't you come in this morning at nine and I'll run some tests. In the meantime, try eating some saltines and ginger ale if you have it."

"Thank you, I'll have Alex go get me some. I'll see you soon."

We hang up, and I text Alex. I know I'm being lazy, but I cannot get up right now, or I might throw up again.

Me: Can you run to the store before work?

Alex: Yes, I'll be right there.

In seconds, he is in the room and at my side. "What do you need?"

"Dr. Stucky said to eat saltine crackers and drink some ginger ale."

"I'll get dressed and run to get those. What time is your appointment?"

"Nine."

He stands from the bed, "Call me as soon as you find out what's wrong."

"I will. I think it's food poisoning. That chicken salad must have been bad."

Alex dresses in record time. "Okay, if it is, you will be down for a few days. I'll pick up something for dinner tonight, don't worry about anything."

"Thank Alex."

He is gone.

Alex

I drop everything off at the house for Emily and check on her one more time before I leave for work. She is so pale. I'm so worried about her.

I make my way to her office to let Jessica know what Emily told me, then head to my office.

The conversation is dragging on, and it is nearly noon, and Emily has not called. I am really getting worried. I nearly call George myself, but he wouldn't be able to give me any information, so that would be a dead end.

At noon, I tell Brandon I am going home to check on Emily. She hasn't called and isn't answering my texts. I am worried and need to see how she is.

Brandon agrees, "Let me know if there is anything Sarah or I can do."

"I will, thanks." I nearly ran to the elevator.

By the time I make it home, my stomach is in knots. Her car is in the driveway, so I know she is home. Why didn't she call me? Damn it!

Running into the house, I see her on the sofa. She's been crying, and there are tissues everywhere. My worst fear imagined is coming true. She has what her mom had: cancer. Shit!

I run to her, pull her into my arms, and hold her. "It's going to be okay. Why didn't you call me? I've been worried sick."

She sniffles, "I couldn't bring myself to call you. I'm sorry Alex, it's worse than I thought."

"We'll get the best specialists out there. We'll beat this thing. We are a team, and we will go through this together." I pull her closer to me and just let her cry for a few minutes. Then I ask, "What did George say?"

Her big, red, puffy eyes look at me with tears flowing down her cheeks. "I'm pregnant."

Epilogue

Two months later

Brandon and I are standing at the top of this beautiful spot just west of Bogus Basin. There is a trellis filled with beautiful flowers, reds, purples, oranges, and tons of greenery. My girl wanted to get married on top of the mountain, and this was as good as I could get.

The day is beautiful. The sun is starting to set in the west. A few people from work are here, and Mom and George are standing on either side of a white satin rug.

Brandon looks at me, "You ready for this?"

I smile bigger than I have ever smiled in my life. "Hell yeah. She's the best thing that has ever happened to me."

He taps my arm and points.

Sarah is walking down the aisle in a red satin dress that comes just above her knees. The music is soft and low, with no words, just a beautiful sound of instruments playing "Beautiful Crazy" by Luke Combs—one of our favorite songs.

Then, the music changes as Sarah takes her place across from Brandon and me. The song "Everything" by Michael Buble' begins.

I look down the makeshift aisle and see the most gorgeous woman I've ever seen. Emily is dressed in a low 'V' cut off-white satin dress that goes to the ground. She's holding a bouquet that matches those in the trellis. Her eyes are glued to mine.

After the initial shock of the news that we were having a baby, I wanted nothing more than to make Emily VanZant my wife. I knew I wanted to marry her, but I hadn't thought that far ahead.

Emily makes it to me; her smile is radiant.

"Hi there," I say.

She giggles, "Hi there."

"God, you are so beautiful."

"Thank you, you clean up quite nice," she's laughing.

I love her laugh.

Brandon and I have on black trousers with matching shoes. My shirt is off-white to match the color of Emily's gown. Brandon's is red to match the color of Sarah's dress. That's about as matchy-matchy as I get.

The minister clears his throat. "Dearly beloved, we are gathered here today to bring together these two beautiful people, in holy matrimony. They have each written their own vows. Emily, you'll go first."

She passes her bouquet to Sarah, takes my hands in hers, and looks me dead in the eye. "Alex, from the day I hired you, I knew you were something special. After a year, I couldn't wait any longer. I needed to know you better and man am I glad I did."

Chuckles come from the audience.

She continues, "I knew our age difference was going to make some people upset. I thought you were not going to even give me the time of day, but you did. From the first kiss to this moment right here, I'm so glad that you did. I know I had some reservations, which I never thought I would, but I'm glad you convinced me that we were meant to be. I loved you yesterday, I love you today, and I will love you forever. You are my everything." A tear slips from her eyes.

I reach up and swipe the tear with the pad of my thumb.

The preacher says, "Alex, it's your turn. I hope you can top that."

Chuckles from the crowd again.

I clear my throat, "Me too, preacher." I look at Emily, squeeze her hands, and start. "Emily, the moment I saw you, I knew you were something special. I was hesitant at first, but age is just a number. Our chemistry is out of this world. I know that we have made it through some tough times so far, and if anything, else comes up, we'll make it through that too. The one thing I know for certain, I love you. I've loved you from the first time I kissed those beautiful lips. My life would not be the same without it. It would be empty, lonely, and miserable. With you, I have a future that is bright and happy. Whether we come upon hard times or not, I'll be by your side. I'll do anything for you. Our love is one that is for the ages. You are my life, you have my soul, and my heart. I will love you now and forever. You are my everything."

The preacher thinks he's a comedian. "Not bad. With that all being said, there isn't much else for me to do. Do you have rings?"

I turn, and Brandon hands me the ring I found for Emily. It's a full two-carat white gold princess diamond centered with smaller diamonds around it.

"Emily, repeat after me, I Emily, take you Alex, to be my lawfully wedded husband."

Emily repeats.

"Alex, repeat after me, I Alex, take you Emily, to be my lawfully wedded wife."

I repeat.

"By the power vested in me by God and the State of Idaho, I now pronounce you husband and wife. You may kiss your bride."

I pull her into me, wrap my arms around her waist, and kiss her like I've never kissed her before.

Her arms snake around my neck, and she kisses me right back.

We hear cheers from the audience. Someone yells, "Get a room."

We pull apart and start laughing. Emily takes her flowers from Sarah.

The preacher says, "Turn and face the crowd. Ladies and gentlemen, I give you, Mr. and Mrs. Alex Bennett."

Everyone claps as we make our way back down the aisle as husband and wife.

The party starts in the Bogus Basin Clubhouse, and we party until midnight.

I look at Emily, "I love you, wife."

"I love you too, husband."

"Are you ready to get out of here?" I take her hands in mine.

"So ready." She turns to Sarah and tells her we are ready to leave.

Sarah says, "Wait, let me get everyone out there. Come out in like five minutes."

Emily shakes her head.

We watch everyone leave the room as Sarah shoos them out the doors.

I look at Emily and say, "So, how does it feel to be married to a younger man?"

"Like a dream. How does it feel to be married to an older woman?"

"Like I might have a few things left to learn." I give her a wicked smile.

"Oh, Mr. Bennett, you are a wicked man."

"I learned from the best, Mrs. Bennett." I kiss her and rub her tiny baby bump. "I'm going to love our family. Thank you."

She puts her hand over mine, "We are going to have the best life. Thank you."

Sarah motions from the door, "Come on."

We stand, move to the doors, and as we walk out, there are streamers, sparklers, rose petals, and confetti being tossed our way or wave around like crazy people.

My mom comes up to us just as we are getting in the car. "Son, I want to say something. I'm very proud of the person you have become. You are the happiest I've ever seen you. Your father would be so proud of you. You two go have some fun and take care of that grandbaby."

We both kiss her on the cheek and hug her. I say, "We will. We'll talk to you in a few days."

She waves as George comes up to her and puts his arms around her shoulders. I think I saw a tear in her eye, no...not my mom.

We hop in the car, and I look at Emily. "Are you ready for the best honeymoon ever?"

"Let's go!"

We are off to Fiji for the honeymoon of a lifetime!

The End

Books by Vic

Girls of Summer
Her Cowboy https://bit.ly/hercowboy20
His Touch https://bit.ly/histouch
Her Strength https://bit.ly/GOSherstrength
Her Hero https://bit.ly/GOSherhero
Her Time https://bit.ly/hertime
Men of Hope
A Forever Kind of Love https://bit.ly/MOHafkol
The Excursion Rescue https://bit.ly/MOHter
His Secrets https://bit.ly/MOHhissec
All Roads Lead to Hope https://bit.ly/MOHarlth
Knight Security
Second Chances https://bit.ly/KS2ndchances
Knight Patrol https://bit.ly/KSknightpatrol
Stand Alones
In His Eyes https://bit.ly/inhiseyes2
Magnolia Cottage https://bit.ly/magcottage
An Unexpected Fling https://bit.ly/AUFling
A Hot Mess https://bit.ly/ahotmess1
Stover Ranch
https://bit.ly/buckstover
https://bit.ly/mitchstover
https://bit.ly/morganSR
https://bit.ly/brockSR
https://bit.ly/jewelSR

About the Author

Vic Leigh is an American Author and has worked in many fields throughout her life. She enjoys reading all authors, but romantic fiction and contemporary romance are her favorites. She is a mother, grandmother, editor, and teacher as well as author. Her small-town romance books are hot, spicy, and addictive. Keep up to date on all things Vic at my website www.vicleighbooks.com[1]